WHERE

Prairie Flowers Bloom

AND OTHER POEMS

YVONNE HOLLENBECK

Dedicated

To my dear friend, Gail DeWitt Sandoz, who personified the true pioneer ranch woman. She was born August 17, 1917, on a ranch in the Nebraska Sandhills. Her mother was very ill after her birth and died when Gail was ten months old. Gail had been passed around and cared for by various neighbors, and after the death of her mother, went to live with her grandparents, the George Fishers, on their ranch. Times were hard and they were poor. Gail desired an education, so worked for her room and board in order to obtain a high school education in Rushville, Nebraska. After graduation, while cooking on a ranch, she attended a barn dance and it was there she met her husband, Allie Sandoz. They married and ranched South of Rushville (in what is known as Sandoz country) and struggled as did many through the great depression. She lost several babies, only successfully delivering one, her son David. They eventually purchased a ranch North of Merriman, Nebraska. When Gail died, a resident of Valentine, Nebraska, on November 18, 2000, she had endured many years of hardship and hard work, only to be one of the happiest and most delightful people I have ever known. She never complained about anything and only saw the good in her life and in people.

I will always cherish her friendship and will forever miss this special person.

Acknowledgments

I wish to thank the people who shared their memories and photographs with me. Our lives have all been blessed by these pioneer women who endured many hardships.

I would like to give special thanks to:

Aplan's Antiques & Art of Piedmont, South Dakota
James & Peg Aplan
Dennis Bammerlin
Ruth Sutton
Gen Fast
Harley Furrey
Betty Kime
Mart & Edna Lawler
Mary Mulligan
Caroline Sandoz Pifer
Dorothy Wales
Jean Reeves
John Rooney, Colonel CAP

Lois Gottsch
Harry Babcock
Doyle Hollenbeck
Evelyn Kendall Schmitz
Royal & Jean McGaughey
The Don Hight family
Jo Ann Klein
Ruthie Harms
Mary Ellen Groff
Russ & June Sorenson
Evelyn Lord Jochem
Peter G. Beeson
Elver Lord, Dec'd
Alan Parker, Dec'd

My parents, Harry & Ruth Hanson; my husband, Glen and his mother, Dema Hollenbeck.

"She had always the power of suggesting things much love-lier than herself; as the perfume of a single flower may call up the whole sweetness of spring."

—Willa Cather in *A Lost Lady*

Table of Contents

Where Prairie Flowers Bloom 1
How Far Is Lonesome 2
The Unsung Heroes 3
That Old Home Comfort Range 6
Saga of the Feed Store Man 8
The Auction Sale 10
Ranch Wife Revenge 13
Don't Wait 17
Plum Blossoms In The Spring 18
Give Your Horse His Head 20
The Pedigree 22
The Old Folks 24
Waiting There At Sunset 26
Baxter's Famous Column 28
The Gospel According to Baxter 30
The All-Around Horse 32
The Affair 34
An Old Fashioned Christmas 36
The Annual Christmas Program 40
Best Gift I've Had In Years 42
Meal Time 44
The Benefit 47
Needin' a Pull 48
Grandma's Homemade Aprons 50
The Cowboy Fashion Show 52
Father's Boots 55
The Christmas Quilt 56
The Depression Quilt 59
The Saddle Tale 60
That Cowboy Touch 62
Dakota's Rose 64
Some Cattle Man 66
Three Payments Past Due 68
Where The Sweetest Grasses Grow .70

Roundup Day 72
Rebel Rouser 74
Saga of the Septic Tank 76
Some Things Never Change 79
Commercial Truckers Can't Be Beat 80
The Cattle Thief 83
How The Poor Folks Are Doing 84
Here To Help Us Out 86
That Little Shed Out Back 88
Mortgage One Good Wife 90
The Little Red Geranium 92
Saga of the Dust 96
Mother's Day Branding 98
The Vocation 101
The Calving Book 103
The Heinous Husband Award .104
Windmill On The Prairie 107
To A Wild Rose 108
The Meadowlark 109

Where Prairie Flowers Bloom

There's a special place I love to go
where prairie flowers bloom;
how I love to see their beauty
and to smell their sweet perfume.
Where the meadowlarks are singing
and the grass is kissed with dew,
as the morning sun is rising
in a sky of purest blue.

You can have your fancy gardens
with the rows of blossoms straight,
laced with walking paths and benches
and arrangements by the gate.
My heart prefers a country lane
that is flanked by prairie sod
...a wilderness of flowers
that were planted there by God.

By Yvonne Hollenbeck

How Far is Lonesome

My mama got a letter from Aunt Jessie yesterday
and she said that it is lonesome where she's at;
you know, I really miss her since she up and moved away;
Mama showed me where she went on our old map.

Aunt Jessie married Hiram and he took her far from me
and it really made me sad she moved away,
'cause she told me I was special & she played with me a lot
but I told her I'd come visit her someday.

I can ride my little pony and I'll take along my doll
so I won't have to make the trip alone.
We will go and visit Jessie and I know that she won't care
if we spend a week or two in her new home.

Mama said she's on a homestead, whatever that might be
and Jessie don't have neighbors where she lives.
Hiram's busy working, so she spends her days alone
and she always seemed to like us little kids.

So, if you'll kindly tell me just how far 'way Lonesome is
I will saddle up and head there yet today;
I'll be riding off to Lonesome where my dear Aunt Jessie is
and I sure hope Lonesome isn't far away.

The Unsung Heros

There are songs that have been written
    that never have been sung;
and many bells of freedom
    that for years have never rung.
But to me, the silent warriors
    whose story sure needs told,
are women of the frontier
    who lived in the days of old.

You will find no marble statute,
    no granite bears their names;
there is little written 'bout them
    but they're heroes just the same.
They helped to carve our future
    and they helped to pave the way
so we could have the kind of life
    we all enjoy today.

They walked along the wagons
    in a strange and foreign land;
and buried babes and loved ones
    in the shallow graves of sand;
They watched 'neath slatted bonnets
    as the places they called home
were left behind, as on they went
    to places yet unknown.

They dreamed of better days ahead
    and worked from sun to sun
providing for a family,
    ...their work was never done.
They're my grandmas and your grandmas
    and other women too,
who sacrificed and did without
    and all for me and you.

I sure hope they're all in heaven
in a special place up there,
reserved for unsung heroes
and for only them to share.
And we never should forget them
though no records bear their names;
and though no one has honored them,
they're heroes just the same!

My mother, Ada "Doll" Hamilton, was a hard working pioneer ranch woman. Can you imagine hauling water and wood to feed and clothe a family of seven? We lived in a sod house; washed clothes on a wash board; burned cow chips, wood and some coal to heat our home and cook meals. We butchered our own animals (cows, pigs, chickens & turkeys) for meat. Mother could pluck six chickens to my one, and she didn't have any pin feathers on hers. I can still taste the fresh homemade bread and butter mother made as our snack when arriving home from school. We walked 2 1/2 miles so we were ready for a snack. In the fall of 1940 the West wall of our sod house fell down. We hung a tarp over the opening and spent two winters without a wall. Mother heated bricks to warm our bed at night. It didn't take us long in the morning to get from the cold bedroom to the round pot bellied stove that mom had kindled with fire. We moved into our new home in 1942 and could enjoy running water, propane heat and electric lights!

Sometimes when I hear people talk about the good old days, I'm reminded of the hardships of the early pioneer women.

—*Jean Hamilton Reeves*
Gordon, Nebraska

Mary Flisram

After establishing a claim South of Bonesteel, South Dakota, my grandparents, Knudt and Inger Flisram, purchased land North of Bonesteel, in Scissons Township. This was located on the West end of the former Mulehead Ranch and is now a part of our ranch where I still reside. Knudt built a crude one room cabin there, housing an old range used for both heat and cooking accommodations. The Whetstone Creekbed was quite deep and Knudt built a swinging bridge over it so he could drive over it. There he raised Hereford cattle and hogs which roamed the creek feeding on acorns. My mother, Mary and her sister Ruth were sent out there during haying season to cook for the men. It was very lonesome out there. They heard the coyotes howl at night and especially disliked the big bull snakes and rattlers that they encountered.

—Ruth Sutton
Bonesteel, South Dakota

That Old Home Comfort Range

Did Grandma ever tell you about that old iron range
    that's out there in the trees behind the shed?
It used to be her cookstove in her kitchen on the ranch
    and I'll bet it baked a million loaves of bread.

She said that Granddad bought it when the two were newlywed
    with money from a Percheron colt he'd sold;
they only had a table and a cot and two old chairs,
    and to them that stove was worth its weight in gold.

Sometimes when I stayed with her she'd let me gather wood
    and put it in the box against the wall;
Usually, I would drop it on the floor and make a mess
    but it never seemed to bother her at all.

Her kitchen was a gathering place for relatives and friends,
    for hired men and neighbors stopping by;
she always had a pot of coffee brewing on that stove,
    was always bakin' cookies, cake or pie.

She'd use a metal handle to remove the burner plate,
    stir the ashes.....add a chunk of wood;
I still can see her cooking on that old Home Comfort Range;
    I'll tell you folks, that food was more than good!

She carried in her water from a well behind the house;
    on Saturday she'd get her washtub down
then heat a bunch of water; everyone would take a bath;
    and later, after chores, you'd go to town.

One night when then had gone to town they heard of R.E.A.
    and Granddad bought her a new electric range;
he thought she would like it and they hauled the old one out,
    but Grandma never took too well to change.

She didn't use it long before her cooking days were done
    and never lived to see how things have changed;
she died a-wishin' she could go back home just one more time
    and cook just one more meal on that old range.

Bill Kayton in door of his Feed Store in Gordon

My grandfather, Bill Kayton, ran a feed store at Gordon, Nebraska, after retiring from the farm and moving to town. At that time, feed came in cotton sacks. He often complained about women coming in to buy chicken feed and always wanting the sack on the bottom because she needed a certain print or color for a sewing project. This is a picture of Grandpa in the doorway of his feed store, and a poem about his complaint.

(You can see the print sacks in the bottom half of the window)

Saga of the
Feed Store Man

The freight train came in yesterday
   with the feed that I had ordered,
so I hired me two extra hands
   to help get it unloaded.

We hauled that feed into my store
   and stacked it neat and high,
the cattle cake and poultry feed
   for customers to buy.

Gosh, we worked 'till well past midnight
   and finally got 'er done;
the store was filled from wall to wall,
   that load was ninety ton.

I 'spose 'cause I had worked so late
   my mood was not the best
when a lady came into my store
   and put it to the test.

She said she needed chicken feed
   but only just one sack;
I grabbed the first one off the top
   of a row of giant stacks.

She said: "I need the bottom one
   ....my favorite shade of red!
I need it for a patchwork quilt
   I'm making for my bed!"

I bit my tongue and went to work
   unpiling all those sacks,
when she spied a better color
   in a stack towards the back.

I'm glad to see those paper sacks
    they are using nowadays,
instead of colored cotton sacks
    of red or blue or gray.

And when you see an antique quilt
    folks love to find these days;
if it is made of feed sack cloth,
    then stop and give some praise

to that poor old feed store salesman
    for the strain upon his back;
obtaining all those pretty prints
    a-lifting those darned sacks!

The Auction Sale

After sixty years of marriage, our neighbor passed away,
    and when they had his auction 'twas a nice and sunny day.
I suppose because it was so nice the crowd was fairly large,
    but I finally found a place to park and walked up to the yard.

The yard was full of furniture and almost everything,
    as the auctioneer, his helpers, and the bidders formed a ring.
I was wanting nothing special, but I thought perhaps I'd buy
    a dish or some momento if things didn't go too high.

Then I saw her in a lawn chair in the shade beneath a tree;
    I thought I'd better say hello, and hoped she'd remember me.
When she saw me walk towards her, she broke out in a smile,
    then took my hand and asked me if I'd sit with her awhile.

Of course, I had intended to get in the bidding war,
    but the lonely look upon her face I'd never seen before.
So, I took the other lawn chair and I asked her how she'd been;
    she said that she was pretty good, but my, how she missed him.

She told me how they came here when they were newlywed,
    then she pointed to a dresser and a pretty iron bed,
saying: "That was our first purchase, and that old cast-iron range."
    Then started telling how things were & how the West had changed.

Next she pointed to a feed bunk full of harness, nets and hames;
    and in it were his saddles; she talked of horses he had trained.
The afternoon went fast and we both shed several tears
    as she told me lots of stories of their many happy years

a-building up this ranch; how she had made a home,
    but today it all is auctioned off 'cause she can't stay alone.
She asked if I'd come visit her; of course, I said I would
    but it seems I keep so busy and don't do the things I should.

A lifetime full of memories were shared with me that day,
   and I hoped that just by listening it'd helped her in a way
to ease the pain she felt inside as all her things were sold,
   while she recounted happy times back in the days of old.

I didn't buy a thing that day and didn't even care
   'cause I got something one can't buy while chatting with her there.
See, I took home something special as I headed on my way....
   ...the blessings of a friendship from the auction sale that day.

Harness, nets and hames are often found in piles at farm auctions and are rarely used today. They were once a necessity when horses were the mode of transportation. Nearly every pioneer woman knew how to harness and drive horses. Above is a photo of a teacher and a load of school children on an outing near Platte, South Dakota.

Ethel Krutzfield of David City, Nebraska,
milking a cow where she found it.

When I was growing up, I had to help my parents and my brother, Glenn, milk cows. We ran twelve to fourteen cows in an 80 acre pasture that was about a mile away from our house. We would put 10 gallon cream cans in the trunk of our 1928 Model A car. It had a pretty good trunk on it. We didn't have a pickup. We had to put kickers on some of the cows, but as a rule we just set down and milked them wherever we found them. When we got home, we separated the milk and took the cream to Ainsworth where we sold it. We used the money to buy groceries and essentials, and usually went to town on Saturday night to do our shopping.

—Dema Hollenbeck
Clearfield, South Dakota

Ranch Wife Revenge

When the frost is on the pumpkin
    and the fodder's in the shock;
it's "Pheasant Season" time again
    and every little shop

stocks their shelves with all the many things
    that pheasant hunters want;
from snacks to beer, to shotgun shells;
    things that's needed for the hunt.

And long about September
    our phone begins to ring;
it's long-lost friends and relatives....
....some we've never even seen!

They start the conversation
    with small talk 'bout their life;
they talk about their children,
    their grandkids and their wife.

And then they pop the question
    in a most creative way;
like: "suppose you'd let me hunt
    some pheasants opening day?"

Now hubby, he's a "softie"
    and against my futile warning,
he says he guess it'd be OK,
    he'll see 'em openin' morning.

The hunter says: "there's one more thing,
    there's this real good friend of mine;
he'd like to come along with me,
    'sure hope you folks don't mind."

Too soon that fatal day arrives
    that this old ranch wife dreads;
I buy the food to feed those men
    and make up all the beds.

Now, remember that first hunter
     who said he'd bring a friend?
He forgot to say the friend had friends
     and folks, that's not the end.

The friend's friend had an uncle
     who brought along his dog;
what was to be two hunters
     now looked more like a mob!

The dog had been to school
     so its trainer came along;
the hunters just kept coming
     and I was wishin' I was gone!

Eleven hunters hit the field
     to shoot those little birds;
it sounded like a war zone
     from the gunshots that I heard.

I fixed a great big supper
     'cause I figured all those guys
would be dog-tired and hungry
     ...was I in for a surprise!

'Cause shortly after supper,
     those hunters, sore and calloused,
decided they would go to town,
     to the little town of Dallas!*

Now, folks I know I'm not real smart,
     but I could not comprehend
what a little dump like Dallas
     had to offer to those men.

But you'd sorta get the picture
     if you seen them late that night;
I won't go into detail
     but it was really quite a site!

The next day's hunt was more subdued
    as the hunters tried again;
the limit was over thirty birds
    but them fellers shot just ten.

Now hunting season's over;
    the "Welcome Hunters" signs are gone;
I think I'll cook some sweet revenge,
    now, please don't take me wrong,

but I guess that I should tell you
    that I followed all those men
to that little place in Dallas,
    and behind them I snuck in,

I took along my camera,
    I sure got some real good shots!
I'll bet when they learn what I did
    those hunters will be shocked!

I have that first guy's number;
    I'm gonna call him on the phone,
and see if we can bring some friends
    and visit in his home;

and have his wife cook us some meals!
    "I wonder how she'll do!"
It'll be me, some friends & hubby;
    ...we might bring a dog or two.

I am sure we'll be real welcome
    and I'll bet they treat us fine,
if I vow to keep my mouth shut
    and leave those photographs behind!

                *denotes "Dallas, South Dakota"

L to R: Marguerite, holding cat; Father, Wm. Patrick Hogan; sister, Hazel; and Mother, Anna Hogan, in front of our new home - 1909

One can about imagine the excitement in having a frame home after living in a soddy. This story is by Marguerite Hogan, mother of John Rooney Colonel CAP of Fremont, Nebraska:

We lived in Perkins County, South Dakota (at that time it was called Bison County) until 1909 when we moved into the town of Lemmon, South Dakota. This was the first place we had our own frame home, brand new. Prior to that we lived in sod houses. I could not go to school for one year because there were not many around. Dad became manager of the Atlas Lumber Company (now Fullerton Companies).

Many times I wish I could have a chance once again to visit my grandparents and hear their stories about the pioneers days. Too often these stories are lost because no one ever took the time to record them or write them down. I was thinking of that when I wrote the following sonnet.

Don't Wait

What happened to her lantern by the door?
The smell of kerosene still lingers on
within my mind, just like a special song
as I recall a time that is no more.
Oh, how I'd love to visit her again;
there are so many questions I would ask
about her recollections of the past;
of births & deaths...the questions would not end.

But here I stand beside a granite stone;
the stories lie with her beneath the sod;
they've vanished like the flesh gone from the bone,
gone with her down the path of life she trod.
The stories, like the lantern flickered out,
and like her soul, they're known only to God.

Plum Blossoms in the Spring

When at first I married this cowboy I had a lot to learn
about the style of life he lives and the money that we'd earn.
We married in the summer and it soon was in the fall
when I thought that I knew everything, was sure I knew it all.

After all I'd drove a tractor and learned to mow and rake
I only wiped two gate posts out but he did not hesitate
to have me checking pastures, even helped him pull a well;
of course we had some arguments, but that part I won't tell.

It soon got close to Christmas, our first one since we'd wed,
and I had hopes for real nice gifts, but I got a card instead.
That winter was a bad one, we got a lot of snow
and seemed like every morning it was at least fifteen below.

I learned to start cold tractors, not a very easy task,
and chop holes in a frozen tank with a dull and heavy ax;
I figured after all this work I'd done through thick and thin,
that I'd get a real nice Valentine, but I was wrong again.

What got me most, a friend of mine got flowers and a ring
(her husband's secret lady-friend received the same darned thing)
and I realized how lucky I was to have the man I got,
'cause we all know in everything the cream comes to the top.

He told me how he hates to shop, and usually short on cash
but to buy whatever I might need and I don't need to ask.
Then I was taken back a bit when he did the nicest thing;
we were really busy calving on a real nice day that spring.

It was getting late that afternoon, when I saw him riding in;
he rode down to the garden where I was and then he grinned.
A big bouquet of plum blossoms he handed me, then said:
"I've never bought you flowers, but I cut you some instead."

Many years have come and gone & I know I've been blessed
to be married to this cowboy 'cause to me he is the best;
though he don't spend money buying gifts and costly things,
he makes me feel real special with Plum Blossoms every spring.

Above: When my husband, Glen, was a young lad, he always rode his horse"Dave" to country school. In 1952, when Glen was 9 years old, he was caught in a sudden blizzard. Fortunately, Dave knew the way home and both arrived safely. (See poem on following page). Here is a photo of Glen and Dave the following spring.

Below: Here's a photo of the aftermath of the Blizzard of '52. Glen's father, Claret, drove him to school until he felt it was safe for Glen to ride his horse again.

Give Your Horse His Head

He would saddle up his pony
   and bundle up real good
then load his gear, check the cinch
   just like every cowboy should.

Then he'd climb up in the saddle
   ...feeling happy, as a rule,
then down the trail you'd see him lope
   a-headed off for school.

His mom would gladly drive him there
   but he did not want that;
he liked to ride his pony
   wearin' boots and cowboy hat.

He loved the birds and animals
   he'd watch for on the way;
besides it did his pony good
   to ride him every day.

Then one day, during recess time
   the sky got dark and gray;
a call came that a real bad storm
   was headed out that way.

The teacher let the children out,
   Little Cowboy headed home;
but soon the snow was blinding him;
   he was out there all alone.

He had soon lost his direction
   and thought he'd got off course,
and knew the only chance he had
   was to trust his little horse.

His mom and dad were worried sick
    all they could do was pray.
Where could their little cowboy be
    as the blizzard raged that day?

They hoped he'd found a neighbor's home
    where he'd be safe and sound;
perhaps he'd stopped at Father Doyle's
    but phone lines were all down.

It seemed like an eternity
    when suddenly they heard
what sounded like a horse outside
    they could neither say a word.

They opened up the back porch door
    and shed some tears of joy;
when they saw that dear old pony
    and their precious little boy.

Now many years have come and gone;
    the little cowboy's growing old,
remembering still that frightful day
    ...the wind...the snow....the cold.

And as we go through life it seems
    there's things that blind our way;
and why we take a dead-end road
    is sometimes hard to say.

But we are all aware that life
    is full of things we dread;
instead of pulling on the reins,
    just give your horse his head.

The Pedigree

I've heard it many, many times
   the lineage from the start
of horses living on our ranch,
   he knows them all by heart;

from King, to Bert, to Tiny Watch,
   he knows them one by one;
foundation lines of every horse,
   their daughters and their sons.

We went to lots of rodeos,
   and when we'd start for home
he'd start reciting mares and studs
   of every horse he'd owned;

and those of other ropers,
   he even knew their lines;
he knew each blasted pedigree
   why, you'd think it'd blow his mind!

One time I was bored to death
   hearing which horse came from who;
I thought I'd catch him up a bit
   ....throw out a name or two.

The first thing that I asked him
   was: "who was Sarah Cowles?"
I knew that really stumped him
   from the wrinkles on his brow.

He scratched his head and thought a bit
   then said: "Now, this is strange;
I know if it's a real good line
   I would recognize the name!"

I told him he should know her;
   what I next said hurt his pride:
"Its your own grandma's maiden name
   .....right there on your top side!"

*Marcia Lord, teacher (back row - left) and her pupils
at a Nebraska Sandhills country school.*

Marcia (Shaul) Lord (1897-1970) was married to Boise Lord in 1917 and was a prime example of the hardy stock of ranch women who lived in the Nebraska Sandhills in the 1900's. She taught one room country schools; was a hard working, family loving, Christian woman; wonderful mother; excellent cook; and helpmate to her rancher husband. As her daughter, Evelyn Jochem, said: "There was not such a word as can't in my mother's vocabulary.....that is, until you tried."

—Evelyn Jochem
Valentine, Nebraska

My mother, Marcia Lord, was an avid Democrat. In the early 30's she bet a load of cow chips with Charlie (C.C.) Bennett, a neighbor man, on the Presidential election. She took Smith and he took Hoover. She lost. Me and my brother, Aubrey, and mom picked up all those chips. After we had the wagon over half full, I said: "that's plenty." She said: "No Way! We're filling it up!" We called those cow chips "Hoover Coal" ever since.

By Elver Lord (deceased)

The Old Folks

The old folks had been gone for years,
    ....the ones who put this ranch together;
they worked through hardship, toil and tears,
    through drought and awful weather.

They passed the ranch on to their son,
    who sacrificed and saved;
and when the place went to his kids
    you might say the road was paved.

Them old folks went to heaven
    and they got a little bored;
they just weren't used to sittin' around
    so they went and asked the Lord

if he'd mind if they returned to earth
    for just a day or two,
and go again to see their ranch
    .....see how the grandkids do.

Well, the Lord said it would be OK
    then tried his level best
to warn them not to be dismayed
    as there'd been changes in the West.

It wasn't long 'till they returned
.....they looked a little sad;
told the Lord that he was right,
the West had got real bad.

Grandpa said: "They've plowed the ranges;
there are fences everywhere;
the corrals are all a-falling down,
they don't even seem to care.

Why, Ma, she went to cook a meal
and went to gather cobs;
she looked the whole place over
but they musta sold the hogs!

The harness wasn't used in years,
the leather cracked and hard;
we couldn't find a milk cow
not even chickens in the yard.

We couldn't find no one at home,
they've taken jobs in town;
they built a great big fancy house
while the barn is falling down.

We didn't see no horses
but we saw the strangest thing;
it was a loud contraption
called an 'all-terrain machine'.

The outhouse, it has disappeared;
the mill's gone from the well;
and we're sure glad we're welcome here
'cause we just came back from hell!"

Waiting There at Sunset

She'd watch each night at sunset
for him a-coming home
and knew when his horse topped the hill
that she'd not be alone.

He'd see her at the window,
then give a great big wave;
then throw a kiss and tip his hat
....he'd do this every day.

She'd told me once she'd always wait
'till he was safe at home
and worry 'bout her cowboy
who would ride those hills alone.

The worst time was in winter
when blizzards hit real fast;
she'd pray until he'd make it home
and pray it wouldn't last

'cause it's hard to find directions
in a snow storm all alone,
but he'd tell her not to worry
'cause a horse'll take you home.

One night she stood there watching,
when a knock came at the door,
with news that after all these years
he'd be riding home no more.

They found him in a washout,
his horse was at his side;
no more to wave his Stetson,
and throw a kiss to his dear bride.

She sits now in her wheel chair
just gazing to the West;
and never misses Sunset time
as she does her level best

to wait for him to top the hill
riding in to take her home;
he'll throw a kiss and tip his hat
...she'll no longer be alone.

Bulah Austin and her horse, "Sweetheart."
Taken in 1925 on her parents homestead North of Malta, MT

Probably the greatest Cowboy Poet ever is Baxter Black, and here are a couple poems I wrote in his honor:

Baxter's Famous Column

A bunch of retired cowboys
    meet at the local Salebarn Cafe;
they gather there on Thursdays,
    that's the weekly cow sale day.

They start their little meeting
    with a shaker and some dice,
to see which one will buy the brew
    and who will buy the pie.

Then they start discussing
    the news, and then the weather;
and then get off on politics
    and get upset together.

Last week we took a cow to sell
    and stopped in there to eat,
but we sorta lost our appetites
    when we heard Al Bolie speak.

First, he had a question
    and discussion got intense,
when he asked "Did you guys see
    this week's *Edge of Common Sense?*"

Well, of course they all had seen it,
    they read it every week;
its Baxter's famous column
    and its revered, so to speak.

He says: "I got the clipping here,
    I cut it out today";
they said they all had read it
    but he read it anyway.

The café that day was crowded
    'cause its sale day and its noon,
as Al began to loudly read
    "*Prolapse From The Black Lagoon*".

Now, I had ordered chili,
    and Glen, a hot beef san;
the waitress just had set it down
    when Al Bolie took the stand.

He read each lurid detail,
    Baxter had not missed a lick;
and as Al read I suddenly
    began feeling rather sick.

I saw Glen was not eating
    and had turned a shade of green,
as we heard the fine-tuned details
    of the slippery slimy scene.

I suppose the biggest reason
    why we both were turning pale
was 'cause that cow we brought to town
    was stitched beneath her tail.

I sure don't mean to put him down
    'cause his writing can't be beat;
but at times the work of Baxter Black
    don't mix well when you eat!

The Gospel According to Baxter

I brought in the groceries...sat down the last sack;
   next came the vaccine; spent big bucks on that!
When you drive fifty miles and that's just one way,
   a trip into town makes a tiring day.

I took off my coat and sat down in my chair
   when I noticed a clipping that this morning weren't there;
It was torn from a paper and taped to the door;
   ...funny, I hadn't seen it there before.

So I started to read it when in came the men
   (they never show up 'till the last sack's brought in)
"Did you see Baxter's column?" Glen said with a smirk;
   "All women should read it, it's a plan that will work

on saving some money and he really makes sense!"
   I knew then and there things were 'bout to get tense.
Seems Baxter'd been batchin' and what he discovered
   was too many dishes and pans in the cupboard.

"You can cook in one kettle, the beef and the beans;
   then just eat from that pan....let the cat lick'er clean.
There's no need for glasses, when you got a tin can;
   you sure don't need silver, that's why God gave us hands.

When they left the house, after coffee and cake,
   and one snide remark about "why'd she use plates!"
They laughed and they chuckled and thought it was funny;
   I'm telling you folks, I know how to save money.

See, I followed 'em out, as they saddled their mounts;
   when they left the barn I started to count
the number of saddles still in the tack shed;
   there were dozens of blankets and things for the head

like bridles and bits, halters, and twitches;
   they shouldn't be worried about all of my dishes!
And speaking of horses, with each man astride,
   there were still twenty horses I counted outside.

The years have passed by but I still get upset,
   when hubby remarks: "It's the best he's wrote yet!"
as he reads once a week what to me spells disaster;
   but to men it's "The Gospel According To Baxter!"

Some of the Whiting children at a school picnic. Holt County, Nebraska

My aunt, Harriet Elizabeth Whiting Whitcher was born in 1881 at Fort Randall, Dakota Territory, and died in 1957. She grew up on her parents farm near Spencer, Nebraska. In 1908 her father started a ranch in Todd County, near Hidden Timber, South Dakota, and she spent much of her time keeping house for her brothers at the ranch. She kept diaries which we have from 1920 until 1957. When the ranch was started, they traveled to Carter for groceries and mail, a distance in excess of 15 miles, which was often a two day trip. Her diary is an endless repetition of cooking, baking, cleaning, washing clothes, ironing and sewing. She also took care of a garden and poultry and all the work associated with that. One entry in 1928 tells of her turkeys wandering off and finally finding all 313 of them. She married Wm Whitcher in about 1917. In 1920 her diary shows prices of two loaves of bread at 22 cents; a pair of suspenders 75 cents; 60 pounds of ice 45 cents; and 100 fence posts at 15 cents each. Her life was not unique and countless women endured the hardships of these times.

—Harley Furrey
Carter, South Dakota

The All-Around Horse

"You say you need a good cow horse?"
    the old horse trader said;
"Well, I might have the one you want"
    adjusting hat upon his head.
"See, I've got a sorrel gelding,
    he's sure easy on the eye,
and he might be just what you want;
    he would fit most any guy."

They strolled out to the horse corral
    and caught this good cow-horse,
and saddled him 'cause we all know
    one should see him work, of course.
The prospective buyer climbed aboard
    as the owner then explained
how anyone can handle him;
    this old horse is darned sure tame.

Then he went right on explaining
    how this horse could work a rope;
how he could stop and back up good,
    and sure has an easy lope.
He said this one is darned sure tough,
    and he sure knows how to cut;
he's got good feet, a nice small head
    and a big well-muscled butt.

"Why, you could even show this horse
    at the local County Fair;
and one like this could win first prize,
    but they're getting kinda rare.
Your wife and kids will love this horse,
    and perhaps the nicest thing
would be taking him to rodeos
    and the money you could win!"

I wondered why he'd sell a horse
    that could just do everything,
when he has a bunch of others
    specialized in just one thing.
I know I should not make remarks
    but I know just what I'd do,
I'd keep this horse that "does it all"
    and sell them other twenty-two!

Many pioneer farm and ranch women never went to town for months, sometimes years at a time, however, peddlers sometimes called on them with their latest wares. Here is a photo of one at the Earl Hollenbeck Ranch South of Long Pine, in the Nebraska Sandhills.

The Affair

He thought that I was sleeping
   when he came sneaking in.
He didn't fool me one bit,
   'cause I knew where he had been.

It's happened several times before,
   but I heard somebody say
that if you just ignore it all,
   then it might go away.

I know he really cares for her,
   I've seen it in his eyes;
and her name is often mentioned
   when he talks to other guys.

Perhaps I should confront him
   next time he's sneakin' out,
and ask him why he slips around
   and what it's all about.

He's spent a lot of cash on her;
   I've never said a word.
When he told me she was special,
   I said: "I know.......I've heard."

I know they used to rodeo,
   that was long before my time.
He said she helped him win a lot,
   that's why he treats her fine.

Last night it finally ended
   when he told me where he'd been.
He said that he was sorry
   and he won't sneak out again.

He left it on the pillow,
   the hasty-written note,
saying: "Dear, I'm out with Cricket
   and she's finally had her colt!"

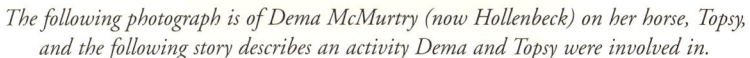

The following photograph is of Dema McMurtry (now Hollenbeck) on her horse, Topsy, and the following story describes an activity Dema and Topsy were involved in.

I grew up in an area called "Buffalo Flats" North of Long Pine, Nebraska. There were many rattlesnakes in that area. I used to ride my horse after the mail and many times I killed rattlers with my bridle reins. I made a necklace out of a lot of the rattles I had cut off the snakes I killed.

—Dema McMurtry Hollenbeck
Clearfield, South Dakota

An Old Fashioned Christmas

I went out Christmas Shopping
    at a great big shopping mall;
there were stores on every side of it,
    even set up in the hall.

I was looking for that perfect gift,
    but things all looked the same;
the clothes and toys and videos,
    and those new 'lectronic games!

And another thing in every store
    that always was the same,
were signs: "Have an Old Fashioned Christmas,
    and Thank You, Come Again!"

Now folks, I'm no spring chicken,
    I seen more than 50 Christmases pass;
and it's not the gifts that mean the most,
    it's all the good memories that last.

Somehow I don't think those merchants
    would not want those signs to be true;
'cause there wouldn't be very much spending
    on presents for me and for you.

I remember an Old Fashioned Christmas
    when we cut down a fresh cedar tree,
and string lots of rose hips and popcorn;
    the trimmings were homemade and free!

It would go up a few days 'fore Christmas.
    Nowadays, just like in this mall,
the trees are all up in October;
    Thanksgiving ain't noticed at all.

And the stockings we hung up on Christmas eve
    were the kind that came off of our feet;
we'd always leave cookies we made with our moms
    so Santa'd have something to eat.

Oh, of course, Santa came every Christmas
    but he'd only bring one special toy,
or maybe a coat or a new pair of boots;
    just one thing for each girl and boy.

And instead of fighting the mobs and the crowds
    in a great big shopping mall;
we'd go to town on Saturday night;
    the local dime store had most all

of anything one could ever want;
    and every one-horse town
was full of friends and neighbors
    who had came from miles around.

The women would trade their cream & their eggs
    for groceries and of course, Christmas candy.
That was the only credit they knew,
    before credit cards 'came easy and handy.

Remember those good Christmas programs,
    at the Church and our old Country School?
The men would stand at the back of the room
    'cause there was a shortage of chairs, as a rule?

And remember how Grandma and Grandpa
    would bring only one gift for us all?
It was usually homemade and practical;
    back then Grandparents didn't buy out the mall.

We didn't have any television,
    so there wasn't no video games;
but we made our own fun, and it seemed that back then
    that the kids were all well entertained.

And that good old Christmas music,
    didn't come from no stereo set;
just dad on his fiddle, a guitar or two,
    but it still was the best music yet.

And speaking of dad, he'd get out the Bible
    and read us that old Christmas story;
it wasn't about elves, or a reindeer and sleigh,
    but it sure filled our hearts with glory.

So, I wish you an Old Fashioned Christmas
    like the signs read all over that mall;
but I wish that somehow we could turn back the clock,
    and have the old fashioned kind after all.

You wouldn't be spending much money;
    nor would there be worry or stress;
and you'd find that an Old Fashioned Christmas
    like the ones I recall would be best!

Alma Swanson Anderson, teacher - Sulphur Creek School;
Meade County, South Dakota - Delany District - November, 1910

My mother, Alma Swanson Anderson, was born in Brule County, South Dakota, in 1884, and homesteaded in Meade County in 1910. She taught at the Sulphur Creek School in Delany District. In June of 1915, she married Alfred Anderson and were the parents of two daughters, Mary Ellen and Isabel, Alfred had first came to what is now known as Jones County in 1893 at the age of 9, with his widowed mother and her family. They settled on Big White River, south of Draper. In the early years, before 1900, there were very few people living on the flats. It was all open range and those were the days of the big cattle drives and roundups. He joined the roundup for the first time when he was 14. He was a member of the Mission Creek Pool, and eventually became a member of the Cowboys of 1902. Alfred and Alma made their home on their ranch on the White River, where she had the cowboys and ranch hands to cook for. She also cared for my widowed grandma (Mary Anderson) who lived with the family and who had became bedfast the last year of her life.

—Mary Ellen (Anderson) Groff
Pierre, South Dakota

The Annual
Christmas Program

Some like a Broadway musical,
    or an evening at the pops,
while others go to Nashville
    and to them it is the tops.

But one thing I'll assure you
    that's much better, as a rule,
it's the annual Christmas program
    at a one-room Country School!

They haul out all the little desks
    and put 'em in a shed;
a stage is made of curtains
    sewn from sheets off teacher's bed.

The kids make all the trimmings
    for the school and for the tree
and display their finest artwork
    for everyone to see.

Then comes that special evening
    we've all been waiting for;
folding chairs and benches
    cover up the hardwood floor.

And every kid has learned their parts,
    they've worked for many days
a-memorizing lines and words
    to poems and songs and plays.

Of course, they're not professionals
    like those in Broadway hits,
but you'll find no better actin'
    than in all those little skits.

And later, when the program's done,
   old Santa makes a show;
he's sometimes just a "look-a-like"
   and someone you should know.

The kids, they all exchange their gifts,
   of course, the homemade kind;
those gifts don't cost no money,
   but no one seems to mind.

And then, to top the evening off,
   we all get quite a treat!
Homemade Christmas cookies
   that the moms have brought to eat.

So this year when you're wondering
   how to celebrate the Yule,
just try the Annual Christmas Program
   at a one-room Country School!

December 30, 1998
   I was born in a sod house near the Niobrara River. We own some of the old place now. We lived in a sod house when dad was foreman of the Half Diamond E Ranch, sixty miles Southeast of Gordon. I rode my Welch Shetland pony to three different sod school houses and burned cow chips.
             —Alan Parker (who died in 2001)
                   Gordon, Nebraska

Best Gift I've Had in Years

When your hubby is a rancher
   and your incomes all from cattle,
you have to cut expenses,
   'cause savings half the battle

and one thing we cut years ago
   was gifts for one another;
with kids to raise and bills to pay
   there was no extra for each other.

But last year I was quite surprised
   when hubby said: "my dear
the cattle markets up a bit
   how 'bout a gift this year?"

He said to drop a gentle hint
   as to what I'd like to have
as he was going into town
   for a load of grain for calves.

There's a jewelry store on Main Street
   with rings of every kind,
and I'd seen one in the window
   that was imprinted on my mind.

So I told him he would see it
   in the window of a store
on a corner there on Main Street
   and I hinted even more;

"It is round, and it is shiny,
   and I've wanted one for ages
then I said this one's on 'special'
   and won't take a whole month's wages."

I then told him it was silver
   'cause he's a little color-blind,
and I sure don't need a big one;
   if it's small, I will not mind.

I knew that it'd be special
   and tears welled in my eyes;
I could hardly wait 'till Christmas
   to see my special prize!

Now, imagine my excitement
    when Christmas finally come;
no gift from him for twenty years
    and now he's bought me one!

Before he went to bring it in
    he stopped and said: *"my dear*
it was more than I intended
    to spend on you this year,

but I know how bad you wanted it
    and you deserve the best one, hon;
they had 'em in three sizes
    I splurged and bought the biggest one.

And I sure do want to thank you
    for describing it to me;
it was right there in the window
    just like you said it'd be."

Then out he went to get the gift
    and imagine, if you can
how shocked I was when here he came
    with a brand new dog-food pan!

He went right on explaining
    (my jaw had hit the floor!)
how it was right there in the window
    of the local Hardware Store.

It was shiny and was silver
    was nice-sized and was round;
and he knew I always got upset
    with the dog a-eatin' off the ground!

Then he said I looked a bit surprised
    ....and he asked me why the tears;
I told him they were happy ones,
    the best gift I'd had in years!

Meal Time

In this world of mass confusion
    and many changes in the land;
the terms that's used at mealtime
    can be hard to understand;

'cause out here in the country
    what we call the food that's served
is not the same way it's described
    by a city persons words.

In the morning we serve breakfast
    and in town they call it *brunch*,
our noon meal we call it *dinner*,
    in the city, it's called *lunch*.

When women in the country
    have to serve the fellers *lunch*,
it is usually cake or cookies
    and is often for a bunch.

Our *lunch* is served with coffee
    about ten or three o'clock,
unless they're driving cattle,
    then you pack it in a box.

Our *dinner's* served at noontime
    but in town it's served at night;
on the ranch at night it's *supper*,
    are you getting this all right?

If you go to town for dinner,
    don't head in there just at noon;
you might not get a meal to eat
    'cause you've got there way too soon.

But if dinner's in the country
    and you don't show up 'till eight,
you just might go home hungry
    'cause you're half-a-day too late.

The Ray Kayton homestead near the Dismal River, South of Thedford, Nebraska.

Emma Vogel was born in 1880 and came to America in 1885 from Germany. She remembered crying when she left her wooden shoes behind. Her family settled near Firth, Nebraska, neighboring the Harms family. She and J. O. Harms were married in 1899 and left a seven room house with a lawn and fruit trees for a two room house with a sod shanty attached, surrounded by sand and infested with sand fleas and rats. It was the Peyton Place South of Valentine, in the Nebraska Sandhills. Upon arrival, with tears in her eyes, she said "Oh Johnny, what have you done to us?" By this time she had seven children, six more were born after coming here. In the early 20's they bought a home in Valentine where they spent the school year and moved back to the ranch during the summer. During World War II, she had five small grandchildren, three in diapers, and their mothers living with them while the fathers were in the service.

—Ruthie Harms
Valentine, Nebraska

Margaret Adams and her friend, Verna Woolf Frauen

Verna Woolf Frauen was born in 1894 and grew up in Manchester, Iowa, where her family operated a green house. She moved to Tripp County, South Dakota, as a teenager, along with her mother and brother. Moving from an affluent home to a one room shanty was only the first of many adjustments she had to make. Word had gotten around that a beautiful single young lady had moved onto the place that bordered the Frauen ranch. Max Frauen decided he wanted to meet this gal before some other fellow laid claim to her. On this barren, dusty plain, Verna found it hard to adapt. Max wooed her for several months, and after asking her to marry him three times, she finally agreed. He promised her that if, after five years, she wasn't happy, that they would move to the city. Verna loved Max and soon learned to love the ranch and the life that he provided for her. Although Verna was a very stylish lady, she learned to do all the hard work that accompanied the life on a ranch. She lived a full and happy life on the ranch, raising a family; and today their MF Ranch is owned and operated by their grandson, Dennis Bammerlin.

—Dennis Bammerlin
Millboro, South Dakota

The Benefit

We are fixin' to host a Benefit,
sure hope that you folks can all come;
it's for poor old Leroy, our neighbor
.....an unlucky son-of-a-gun.

We'll have a pie and soup supper,
there'll be a raffle or two;
the Lutherans are matchin' the money we get
Modern Woodman Insurance will too.

I suppose you have heard of his troubles,
it happened six years ago;
loading up meat at the packin' plant
when a push-cart ran over his toe.

He was diagnosed: "Total Disabled",
he never will work anymore;
with three little kids, one more on the way
why, the oldest one's just barely four.

And you know with the high cost of livin',
disability never goes far;
with payments so high on his new pickup truck,
he barely can gas up his car.

His horses need pasture and shoein',
his steers all need grain and good hay;
with luck we can raise him some money
....the benefit's next Saturday.

Just in case you don't know him, I'll tell you
he's a good guy......never does dope;
he's a clean-livin' talented fellow,
and boy, old Leroy can rope!

Needin' a Pull

It was only two days before Christmas
    and the whole darned place was a mess;
I was cooking and cleaning and doing up beds
    we were expecting a whole bunch of guests.

When all of a sudden Glen burst in the door
    saying "I know that your workload is full,
but the tractor won't start and I was a-wondering
    if you'd have time to give me a pull."

I'd like to ignore him but I wouldn't dare
    'cause the cattle need caring for too;
so I put on my chore coat to go help him out;
    that's what any good ranchwife would do.

There is one thing a cattleman hates the worst;
    there's one thing that drives him mad;
it's a tractor my friends, and when it won't start
    it makes life on a ranch really bad.

It can happen most any old time of the year
    but today it is fifteen below;
when the call comes in that the tractor won't start,
    the ranchwife had better well show.

If you think that the signals he gives with his hands
    when he's sorting off cows is a test;
you wait 'till that tractor won't start some cold morn
    and you'll learn a new meaning for "stress"!

He hooked a log chain to the old cakin' truck
    then he climbed up aboard his John Deere;
I thought he was ready when I heard him explain:
    "clutch 'er slow....and start out in low gear".

So I reved up the engine and let the clutch out,
    then suddenly I heard a loud bang!
The tires were spinning as dirt and snow flew,
    then I heard a long string of profane!

I don't know what happened as I looked to the rear
    he was picking himself off the ground;
I dare not repeat what the poor guy said next.
    He was really upset, from the sound.

He repaired the log chain that somehow got broke
    then he hollered to try it again;
this time I checked to make sure he was ready
    and was careful to try not to spin.

We went down the lane, still hooked to the chain
    that tractor wouldn't sputter or cough;
his arms fanned the air.....he continued to swear,
    then hollered: "head back to the shop!"

When we got to the shop, his mood was not good,
    and I probably should never have asked,
'cause it sure made him mad when I asked if he had
    checked to make sure he had gas.

I dare not repeat just how he replied
    but my job helping him ended there;
I went back to the house and back to my work
    but there was a new chill in the air.

Now there's things on the ranch that will drive you berserk
    but the absolute worst thing of all,
is when a tractor won't start and he's needin' a pull
    and you're the only one there for the call.

Somehow he got that old tractor started
    and our Christmas that year turned out fine;
and he still comes to get me when he's needing a lift
    and I'm glad to help out.... most the time

but I sure dread the winter 'cause I know it is coming
    when it snows and it's fifteen below;
that he'll burst in the door and tell me the tractor
    won't start, and he sure needs a pull!

Grandma's Homemade Aprons

I remember Grandma,
   and I guess I always will;
I remember how she welcomed me
   to her house up on the hill;

Her homemade pies and cookies
   were the best I've ever ate
and I loved her pansy garden,
   and the roses by her gate.

But the one thing I remember
   most about those days of yore,
was the homemade gingham aprons
   that my Grandma always wore.

All the grandmas wore them;
   be they slender gals, or fat;
those aprons kept their dresses clean
   but they were more than that.

They always had a pocket,
   where she kept her handkerchief,
and a peppermint for grandkids
   and she'd wipe our little cheeks

with the tail of that old apron,
   when a tear would happen by
from a fall or from a skinned up knee
   things that'd make a young one cry.

She'd gather up the ends of it,
   and use it for a bag
when picking garden produce,
   even used it for a rag.

She made her pretty aprons
　　from feed sacks she had picked
when buying special chicken feed
　　or starter for her chicks.

What happened to those aprons?
　　No one wears them any more;
those homemade cotton aprons
　　that our grandmas always wore.

I was born near Meeteetsie, Wyoming. We moved a lot when I was young. My dad was getting started in ranching. We lived near Thermopolis, then Sheridan, then Arvada on the Powder River. One time mom and dad were milking a bunch of cows to keep things going. Mom (Elizabeth Babcock) was milking a cow that kicked and got its foot in her apron pocket and got her down. She didn't get hurt and always talked and laughed about it.

　　　　　　　　　　　　　—Harry Babcock
　　　　　　　　　　　　　Ainsworth, Nebraska

The Cowboy Fashion Show

As cowboys head toward my kitchen
   after branding calves today,
my front porch takes resemblance
   of a fashion show runway.

First comes a short young cowboy,
   I think his name is "Lance",
he's in a blue BUM tee-shirt
   and some denim wrangler pants.

He wears a pair of tennis shoes
   a weathered baseball cap;
Thank-you Lance and here we have
   another well-dressed chap.

Charles wears a striped shirt
   stretched over his spare tire;
a pair of lace-up ropers is
   his choice of foot attire.

Again, a pair of Wranglers
   are the pants he chose to wear;
(they would look a bit more comfy
   if he'd buy a bigger pair)

Here comes handsome Richard
   with a shirt that's starched and clean;
his nice physique accentuates
   the way he wears his jeans.

His choice of boots are Justins;
   his hat a twenty-X
that matches leather trimming
   on his custom hand-made vest.

Finally comes the last one,
   my...his wife must never patch
'cause he has two buttons missing
   and a tear across the back.

His poor old hat is filthy
    and is badly out of shape.
His boots would be in pieces
    if it wasn't for Duct Tape.

His Wranglers, they're all bloodstained;
    he must have been the one
that did the castrating
    the job that is no fun.

Then I recognize the buckle,
    "Champion Roper '64"
Why, it's Glen, my dear sweet husband
    that comes walking through the door!

Getting Dinner!

One of Andrew Hollenbeck's sons cutting sod for a new dwelling.

My mother, Maude Maria Hagerty, was born in 1875. She married my father, Joe McGaughey, in 1894. We lived 3 miles from Wisner, Nebraska. Dad had large work mares that he bred to a Hamiltonian trotting horse stallion, and produced fast teams. If a surgeon was needed the local doctor called for one at Fremont and he came down on the train. Dad brought him out in the buckboard. We had the operating table at our house - just a board table. Mother held the kerosene lamp while the doctor operated. At different times, three of her sons were operated on for appendicitis.

She held the lamp when a neighbor boy, Graden Page, died from a burst appendix during surgery. She didn't have running water in the house in the early 1900's. On wash day, she washed at the windmill. Benny, just 2 years old, took his little bucket and was making mud pies. He was getting a bucket of water and fell in. Mother had looked another way, but was unable to revive her young son. Besides Benny, mother's son, Bill, was killed when kicked by a horse in 1926. Her husband, Joe, died in 1936. Three words would describe her: the lovingest, workingest, and prayingest woman I ever knew. She died at 88 years.

—Royal McGaughey
Gordon, Nebraska

Father's Boots

I like to wear my father's boots
    and act just like him too;
'cause he is just the nicest guy
    a feller ever knew.

He lets me go outside with him
    and help him do the chores;
he's showed me how to swing a loop
    and ride my little horse.

I hope when I am all grown up
    his boots will fit me then;
'cause if I am a father too
    I'd like to be like him!

Glen Hollenbeck, age 3 (1945) - in his dad's boots.

The tragedy that hit our nation on September 11, 2001, together with the 60th Anniversary of the attack at Pearl Harbor, which happened on December 7, 1941, reminded me of the sacrifices made on behalf of all of us. Many people have died for us and because of us. The most important death on our behalf occurred over two thousand years ago, and that is the reason we celebrate the Christmas season. I had this in mind when I wrote the following poem.

The Christmas Quilt

The first time that I saw it I was pro'bly five years old.
In fact, I don't remember it, but that's what I've been told.
My grandma started piecing it some time 'fore I was born,
and always got it out to show us all on Christmas morn.

You might call it a tradition just within our family;
each year she'd take it from the trunk for all of us to see.
She'd tell us 'bout each little star that centered every block,
how she sewed 'em all together to form the pretty top.

She'd tell about the first star that she made one winter night
while thinking 'bout her sailor son; her heart was filled with fright.
T'was late on Christmas Eve......she was lonely as could be;
and he was half-way 'round the world on a ship upon a sea.

Then thoughts came of another boy, born this very night;
and pointing to his birthplace was a great star shining bright.
He was born there in a stable to save us all from sin;
She prayed he'd bless her sailor boy and please watch over him.

Then she took a scrap of fabric from her boy's favorite shirt
and cut a star-shaped pattern, and then she went to work.
She made the first of many blocks that very Christmas eve;
it gave her peace to sew the stars from scraps of memories.

Like prints from mama's dresses; some from grandpa's clothes,
while others came from feedsacks she'd been saving I suppose.
A little blue checked star was from a tiny baby dress;
it died so many years ago.....her favorite I would guess.

When she got the blocks completed she'd made just forty-eight,
 the same as those upon the flag of our United States.
The hours she spent a-quiltin' it helped pass her time alone
 while waiting for her sailor boy to make it safely home.

She put a label on the back, then packed the quilt away;
she'd give it to her fine young lad when he returned one day.
The label said: "This Quilt was made for Christmas '41;
'twas made with love to let you know I'm proud you are my son."

Then came the tragic message that her son would not come back;
his ship was at the harbor when the Japanese attacked.
The quilt was left in her old trunk, along with several more,
 a folded flag, a purple heart, and clippings of the war.

Exactly ten years later, Christmas morning, '51......
the first time that she showed us all the quilt she'd made her son.
She told us all the story about making every block;
she sure stitched a lot of memories in every piece of cloth.

Many years have come and gone and Grandma's with her son,
my grandpa and her baby; her life on earth is done.
But every year at Christmas, that quilt is 'neath our tree
.....a reminder of the sacrifices made for you and me.

I think of that first Christmas and the humble manger scene,
and like her precious sailor boy, Christ died to set us free.
Forgetting the true meaning of the season brings me guilt,
 but I always am reminded when I see her Christmas Quilt.

L to R: Frances Creech; my great-aunt Fanny Hookstra; my great-grandmother Minerva Kayton; great-aunts Edith Small holding her son, Maurice; Maude Kayton & Clara Larson. The two little children in front are Erma Small and Elliott Larson. Elliott, wearing a little sailor suit, grew up to become a Sailor in the U.S. Navy and was killed in WWII when his ship was torpedoed in the English Channel. His only sister Evelyn's husband, William Kendall, was also killed in WWII in a plane that was hit by enemy fire. (The following story is by Evelyn)

I remember my Mom (Clara Larson) going out with her own corn pickin' wagon and team AFTER cooking for six or seven people on a wood burning stove; no running water; and doing up the dishes, getting Elliott and I off to school; then coming in to gather eggs, help with milking, cook a big meal again, and do dishes again. I've never in my life complained about how hard I worked because I really didn't work hard at all, and I really get upset when I hear other "city gals" gripe about their difficult lives.

—Evelyn Kendall Schmitz
Denver, Colorado

My mother was born and raised in Dundee, Illinois. Her father had a hardware store. My dad was also from Illinois and came to the Nebraska Sandhills in attempt to regain his health from TB. My mother went through the usual trials attributed to the Depression and in addition, had rheumatic arthritis. Movement was difficult; things in the house were neglected; water works failed; no coal for furnace, only cow chips; cattle prices dropped to nothing. Like everyone else, they managed to make it through the Depression. Coming from Illinois, she often told me she missed the trees and hated the wind blowing all the time.

—Betty Sawyer Kime
Valentine, Nebraska

The Depression Quilt

I lift the quilt so gently from the chest
and spread it out upon the bed with care;
perhaps to hide the memories it possessed,
for many years she kept it hidden there.
The scraps of calico and work shirts blue,
the tiny, stamp-size pieces of their lives
pieced all together, tell a story true
of years of hardship, poverty and strife.

She told me once of how she sewed the scraps
at evening when a long day's work was o'er;
of sharing space with babies in her lap,
....reflections of a time that is no more.
I'm proud to put this heirloom on display
In tribute to those hard depression days.

Marvin Williams, a retired rancher from White River, SD, asked me to write a poem for his daughter, Karen, to be used for a Christmas gift. He furnished the facts, and I wrote the following poem.

The Saddle Tale

There's a weathered, high back saddle on a rack out in a shed,
 and I know you think it silly that I keep it there instead
of throwing it away, 'cause it's seen its better days,
 but I think that it is priceless in so many, many ways.

I bought that Beckwith Saddle back in '48 one day
 from some money I have saved up from a measly soldier's pay;
I broke a lot of colts on it and rode it many miles,
 and the memories of that saddle always seem to bring me smiles.

The years we spent together were the best years of my life,
 just me and that old saddle, my four kids and my wife.
I remember when a baby, I would bounce you on my knee
 and often in that saddle you would ride in front of me.

You used to chew that saddle horn just like a teething ring,
 and you'd pretend to rope the cows by twirling saddle strings.
By the time you started school you would ride behind the tree;
 we sure put a lot of miles in that saddle, you and me.

It seemed like it was no time when you liked to ride alone,
 and you'd always rather work outside than help your mom at home.
Now you kids are all grown up and I'm proud as I can be
 to be a part of all your lives....it means a lot to me.

This saddle's like a special friend that means much more than gold.
 One don't throw a friend away, just because they're growing old.
And when my days are over and I cross the big divide,
 I hope I'm in the saddle when I make my final ride.

Pioneer Women had to contend with many obstacles,
one of which was the Prairie Rattlesnake.

There are a lot of gals on the ranches that can do most anything as good as any cowboy. I am not one of them, and firmly believe that there are many jobs that are better off left to the men. One of the reasons I believe this, resulted in the following poem.

That Cowboy Touch

Now, I know that some ladies will stand here and tell you
    they can do anything like a man;
they can tame wild horses and ride herd on cattle
    and I'm sure there are women that can.

But for most of us ranchwives, we're busy with duties
    like cooking and cleaning and such;
though we are eager to help when we're needed,
    we just don't have that "Cowboy Touch".

I've learned a few lessons from the "school of hard knocks"
    last year on the 13th of May;
the men were a-fencin', I was left with the springers
    to check 'em and feed 'em some hay.

The day was a nice one, I was goin' to plant garden
    and mow up the lawn, and plant flowers;
but I thought I had better go check on those springers
    'cause they hadn't been checked for four hours.

Now, down in the corner of our big calving lot
    was this cow, Number three-seventy-one Green;
she was calving all right, with the head coming straight,
    but only one foot did I see.

So I went for the neighbor, he came right away
    to help me deliver that calf;
but she was a woman - in labor, and cranky,
    and she was to have the last laugh.

After one hour, we finally corralled her
    and into the Calving Shed she went;
but she was a "mad one", and where was "Old Ophra",
    she could learn what "Mad Cow Disease" meant!

The next thing I knew, she had rammed a pipe panel
    and that panel hit me in the head;
the blood was a-gushin', Duane came a-rushin'
    to see if this old gal was dead.

We left that old cow in that shed throwing tantrums
    and off to the doctor we flew;
and I spent most the summer with a knot on my head
    and a face that was all black and blue!

But I sorta remember, as we were leaving the shed
    that cow looked at me and she grinned;
but folks, I got even last fall when he culled cows,
    on the sale list her number I penned.

I was there at the Sale Barn when the gavel went down,
    then I strolled out by the Packing Plant's pen;
I was holding a check that was made out to me
    and when she looked at me, I grinned.

But I will admit when there's tough work to do
    most us women had better concede:
there are jobs on the ranch that the men can do better,
    and I guess that's the way it should be.

Like I say, most us ranchwives are better with duties
    like cooking and cleaning, and such;
and there are some jobs we should leave to the menfolk,
    'cause we don't have that "Cowboy Touch"!

CALAMITY JANE AT
WILD BILLS GRAVE
JULY 1908

Many tales have been told about the legendary Calamity Jane—
a well known South Dakota pioneer. This is another one.

Dakota's Rose

She came to South Dakota when the Plains were wild and free
and the hills were full of miners, as for gold they came to seek.
It was not a woman's world unless she was double-tough
as camps were full of whiskey-drinkin' men, both mean & rough..

Other women, they despised her; they often called her "tramp"
as she hung out with the fellers in those wild & wooly camps;
and the one that really hated her was Mrs. Hiram Brown
who'd came there from New York and wed the banker of the town.

Did Mrs. Brown dislike her 'cause Jane dressed like a man,
and had a reputation that was talked of in this land?
Or did she just not like her 'cause she thought that she was nicer
than the poor old orphaned Jane, and decided she despised her.

Legend tells a story that the fancy Mrs. Brown
had a feller that she'd meet at night, past when the sun went down.
And this lady with the money and the mansion on the hill
would let her hair down when she'd go to meet this fellow, Bill.

Perhaps that's why she hated Jane and scorned her very soul,
'cause Jane and Bill were lovers as the story then unfolds.
They both were taken back a step in 1876
when a man rode into Deadwood with an iron on his hip

and over just a card game, the gunman shot their Bill;
now he sleeps at Mount Mariah in a grave up on that hill.
They both, at different times, would go to his grave and weep
and bring flowers they had picked and lay them at their lovers feet.

It was only two years later, when the gold camp where they lived
was the scene of dreaded smallpox, killing women, men and kids;
and the outcast Jane administered to the sick and dying;
day and night she fought their plight.....never gave up trying.

Poor old Mrs. Brown was lying in her final state
in her fancy big old mansion with the flowers by the gate.
The only one to help her was the one she called a "tramp";
Jane cared for her both day and night in this wretched mining camp.

Before the wealthy bankers wife inhaled her final breath,
she took Jane's weathered hand and held it tightly to her chest,
and told Jane she was sorry for scorn she had imposed,
that the world was full of flowers but to her Jane was a rose.

Of course we all are well aware that roses do have thorns
we also know a crown of thorns the Christ Himself has worn;
but in everything there's beauty.....we must not blame or tout,
 for the one we hurt the most in life may come to help us out.

Now Jane lies in the graveyard 'neath the pines up on the hill
overlooking that old mining camp beside her precious Bill;
and though you hear the stories and many questions you may pose,
there is one final outcome.........this lady was a rose.

One of the finest ranch couples in South Dakota is Don and Adeline Hight of the White River area. After the tragedy of September 11, 2001, I heard about something they did that prompted the following poem.

Some Cattle Man

He never has been to New York City,
   he's rarely been off of his place.
You can count the years he's been ranching
   by the wrinkles and lines on his face.

He's never been one to brag or to boast
   'bout what he's accomplished in life;
he's run his ranch by himself all these years
   along with a hard-workin' wife.

There's no fancy mansion high on a hill,
   his car is an old pickup truck;
a good pair of boots and clean set of clothes
   is the way that he dresses up.

You'd think he was poor, the way that he lives,
   but rich if you count all his friends;
eager to help anybody in need,
   and prob'ly will up to the end.

He went to the Fort Pierre salebarn one day;
   .....walked up to the office gal's desk,
told her he'd brought in a hundred good calves
then told her to make out the check

to those in New York, who's lives had been torn
   to shreds by the ravage of terror.
He said to buy beef, it's something they need;
   and let 'em know somebody cares.

Then one more request was made 'fore he left,
    he sure hoped that she'd understand;
to not give his name if anyone asked,
    just say it was "some cattle man".

Wouldn't the world be better today?
    There'd be peace in all of the land;
if everyone lived by the code of the West
    and all were like this cattle man.

As the poem states, Don has had by his side a fine, hard-working wife. As is the case with many ranchers, they sometimes play a practical joke on that wife. The following story was related to me by their son and daughter-in-law:

The Hight family was weaning buffalo calves on a fall day when luck would have it that one of the biggest bulls got into a raucous with another bull and broke his back. When Adeline asked Don what he was going to do with it, he jokingly told her that she would have to haul it to Sturgis to the Locker Plant (175 miles away). Being a good ranch wife, she did what she was told. She got her pickup ready, so Don, being in this precarious position, loaded the huge bull into the back of the pickup with the loader of his tractor. Adeline took off for Sturgis with this bull sitting in the back of her pickup truck. The bull wasn't able to move much since his back was broken, but when he did try to stand up, Adeline would just hit the brakes and knock him down. Now, the crew had lost their cook, so they went to town to have lunch, when they overheard two truck drivers talking about that crazy old woman on the interstate with a buffalo in the back of her pickup. It took Don several years to finally confess to Adeline that he was only kidding when he asked her to take that trip.

—Dan & Vanessa Hight
White River, South Dakota

Three Payments Past Due

She wanted to marry a cowboy
but nobody warned her
...guess they thought she knew
that she'd have to work, a good paying job
and do without!
She thought 'cause he drove a new pickup
that rodeos paid well.
But fellers who golf and play pool
have full-time jobs through the week,
most rodeo cowboys don't.
The day that they went through Divorce Court
she got the pickup.
The payment book showed three payments
past due.

In our "Honyoker Days" we not only worked hard, but enjoyed many good times also. Everyone was friendly and we all joined in to make life happy and as good as possible. We had dances in our little houses; there was always someone with a fiddle. We made big pots of coffee, and friends always brought sandwiches and cake. Mostly we danced until just time to go home for morning chores. We had other entertainment too, like card parties, amateur plays, and so on.

—Pearle McMurty Puppmuller
(an early Meade County, SD, homesteader)

A Pioneer Mother and Daughter

My mother, Inez Rieke, was born near VanHorne, Iowa, July 4, 1892. She married Olin Ravenscroft in 1911. They had six sons and then two daughters. Where does a mother go when things fall apart? On two occasions I saw my mother cry. It was the Depression, and we arrived from Iowa to the Sandhills, Southeast of Dunning, to Wild Horse Flats - to a Sod House with one wall slid into the bedroom. She had come from a new house to barren hills. She sat on her suitcase and only her daughter saw the tears. I was four years old. The other time was when I was around 14 years old and haying was over the day before. She let me ride my horse home to spend the night with Dolly Swanson. We had cooked for 20 to 30 people working or visiting all summer long. What a lot of food and dirty dishes we had been through that summer. I just rode in, put up my horse and visited with Mother about my night away, and she told me we were down to just our family for dinner, when we looked out and there drove in a car load of cattle buyers. Mother rushed into her bedroom and cried. I met the lady and took her to the front of the house until Mother could get through her shock. We had chopped canned beef which we opened and dinner was nearly ready. One summer we canned 1,000 quarts of meat and vegetables. We were really tired ladies.

—Jean Ravenscroft McCrory McGaughey
Gordon, Nebraska

On July 4, 2001, Kyle Evans was killed in a tragic accident near his home at Wessington Springs, South Dakota. Kyle, known as the South Dakota Troubador, was a well-known entertainer and a dear friend to my husband and I. The following two poems were written as a tribute to Kyle.

Where the Sweetest Grasses Grow

There's a special place in heaven
   where the sweetest grasses grow;
where the cowboys all are gathered
   and he's with them there, I know.
It must be quite a roundup
   as they gather in the strays;
but down here there's lots of sadness
   since our friend has gone away.

A voice that sang sweet melodies
   is now forever still;
and all of us sure miss him
   but it was the Masters will.
He was always on the roundups
   and was with the wagon train,
but he's riding now in heaven
   and down here it's not the same.

He was never known a quitter
   and was never short of try
and he answered every calling
   with the will of do or die.
But is was his songs of horses
   and the wide Dakota plains
that will always be remembered
   and we'll miss those sweet refrains.

He sang of lonesome cowboys,
   of a love that had gone wrong;
and he honored Vern and Casey,
   ......wrote 'em each a special song.
He sang "Driftwood On A River"
   and did gospel songs, of course;
but everybody's favorite was
   "In Heaven On A Horse".

He's now in Heaven on a horse
   where the clear spring waters flow;
pro'bly resting in the saddle
   as soft breezes gently blow.
But we'll keep the campfire burning
   'till its time for us to go
to be part of heaven's roundup
   where the sweetest grasses grow.

Kyle's casket was transported to a country cemetery near his hometown of Wessington Springs, South Dakota, via a horse drawn hearse. It was accompanied by an entourage of mounted cowboys, one leading Kyle's saddled and riderless horse. This was certainly proper and fitting for this man who lived, wrote and sang the life of cowboy. The following photograph reminds me of that sad day.

Burial of Israel Calkins; January 1915 - Erskine Cemetery

The following poem (Roundup Day) was written at the request of, and with the assistance of Jim Thompson, who delivered it as a part of the eulogy at Kyle's funeral:

Roundup Day

There's a heap of tears and sadness in Dakota-land today
since we heard the tragic news that 'ol Kyle passed away.
There's a voice now stilled forever that we all had grown to love,
 now he's singing at the campfire with the cowboys up above.

I can see 'em now all gathered at the wagon by the fire
where the grass is green and lush, with no sign of post or wire.
I'll bet those guys are happy to hear him sing his songs;
it must be some reunion...seems the best ones have gone on

like his buddy, Harold Heinert; and his hero, Casey Tibbs
(Dakota's greatest cowboy we've all idolized since kids);
Doug Hansen and Jack Hunter, and C. L. Johnson too;
why the cowboys who are gathered were rodeo's "Who's Who"!

Erv Korkow came to greet him and James Sutton was along;
he got to meet Vern Whitaker, who he'd eulogized in song.
Dale Barber & Wayne Cornish, two guys who'd paid their dues,
and young ones like Jade Mortenson were gathered up there too.

When the Lord calls home a cowboy, he must pick the very best
'cause Terri Sutton Melvin sure would put 'em all to test;
and Gabby Moon was there along with other folks I knew,
Gene Madison and Harley Roth.....Bat Ridley was there too.

You can bet when he is singing with 'em gathered at the fire
he is joined there in harmony with his friend, T. Texas Tyler;
and "Little Tin Horn Hank" will be sitting by his side
as will many other cowboys who have made their final ride.

When I heard that he had left us and I bowed my head and cried
it was like the world stopped turning and as if the music died.
Then I realized the Lord had only loaned him in way
and he had to call him home to sing at Heaven's Roundup Day.

Just to think of all these cowboys, I cannot help by yearn
for the day when more are called up there and it will be my turn;
and I hope that I am worthy and my sins are washed away
and I'll join 'em at the campfire on that final roundup day.

(and as a post script, the following two verses were added April 11, 2002)

And just when we were thinking that the best ones had gone on,
the Lord called T. C. Holloway to join that special throng;
then sent Mikayla Norton, as precious as could be
and you can bet she's proudly sittin' there on Kyle's knee.

And even though we miss them so, we must not question why
the Big Boss called them up to that great roundup in the sky.
It looks like all the best hands have gone on to pave the way
in hopes that we will join them on that final Roundup Day.

Rebel Rouser

Perhaps it was the winter that was bad and took its toll,
or maybe turning fifty made him 'fraid of growing old.
Whatever caused the problem that was lodged between his ears,
the whim that overtook him nearly drove his wife to tears.

It started one cold day last spring while sorting off some cows
and when they broke for coffee, and headed for the house,
he told her he was thinking how they both could use a break;
he'd thought a nice vacation is something they should take.

The first thing that she thought of was he'd probably want to go
to Cheyenne or to Deadwood to some blasted rodeo;
but he said that come next August, when the haying is all done,
that he'd like to go to Sturgis and take in all the fun.

He said he'd heard folks talking 'bout the rally and the hogs,
the concerts and the people, why they say they come in mobs.
The first thing that she asked him was how on earth they'd go
'cause a ten year old Ford pickup just might not fit that show.

He told her not to worry, that he knew just what to do
'cause he found a motorcycle that was just as good as new.
It was in the want-ad section in a paper that he'd saw;
eight hundred dollars wasn't much for a good used Yamaha.

He bought that good used cycle, and he broke 'er in real good
he'd drive around the barnyard & the whole darned neighborhood.
Then he welded up a trailer in his shop one rainy day
so they could haul their tent along and have a place to stay.

She thought that he had lost his mind, but it got worse than that
when he started growing whiskers & his hair hung down his back.
He said he had to look the part so he would fit right in,
and told her she should wear some clothes that show a little skin.

They say she almost killed him with the look upon her face,
but it seemed like it was no time when she would take her place
behind him on that Yamaha, the trailer hooked behind
and off they went for Sturgis like the blind leading the blind.

They hadn't gone an hour on the seven-hour trip,
  when it seemed like rigormortis had just settled in her hips.
The sun was bearing down and her skin was turning red,
while thoughts of home & airconditioner was fogging up her head.

The trip they'd barely started had begun to take its toll
  when she got that awful feeling of a bladder getting full.
This sure was no vacation, a worse time she'd never had,
and she never knew a sweaty shirt could ever smell so bad.

The blowing locks of hubby's hair was all that she could see
and anywhere besides that bike is where she'd rather be.
The temperature was hotter than a bakery oven door;
...not even bearing children made her body feel so sore.

She begged to go back home, but her voice, he never heard,
and he never would have stopped if it wasn't for that bird
that hit him in the face just West of Belvidere;
it was there that he discovered her no longer in the rear.

They say a trucker found her when he stopped to check his load,
she was lying moanin', groanin' in the ditch beside the road.
At first he was real startled 'cause he thought she might be dead,
but the only thing that hurt her was a bump upon her head.

When her hubby found she'd left him, he at first went into shock;
'till he met this little dolly workin' in a tattoo shop.
They say he gave up ranching for his cycle and this dame
and he never works a lick, but the pay's about the same.

The wife is with the trucker and they make a happy pair
though she's still receiving treatment under psychiatric care.
They're both truckin' for a sawmill in the mountains hauling logs,
and are known to run down cycles, ...especially "Yamahas".

The moral of this story is in case you need a break
and decide to go to Sturgis, you should not make this mistake.
If you want to save your marriage, you should make the trip alone.
Just let this be a warning gals...leave your husbands home!

Saga of the Septic Tank

It was early in the morning
   on the second day of May;
I was up a-workin' early
   'cause it was "Cleanin' Day".

I had a lot of laundry
   and some soiled floors to clean;
with a load of dirty rugs
   I headed for my wash machine.

But in my fast descent
   I left the final basement step,
and something felt quit different;
   I had stepped in something wet!

It seems an inch of water
   was on the basement floor
the floor drain wasn't draining;
   I was standing there in horror!

I called my favorite plumber
   and my heart, it really sank;
when he told me he would have
   to come and pump the septic tank!

I hollered at my hubby
   (I hollered not too nice)
who said he'd dig it out himself
   and save the awful price

they charge to do the digging;
   then he went and found a map
the location of the septic tank,
   to find where it was at.

With his John Deere and a loader
   he commenced to moving dirt;
"it won't take long and once again
   we'll have some drains that work!"

With tears I watched the lawn
    that I had planted disappear;
as I saw him digging deeper
    with his trusty old John Deere.

At suppertime he told me
    he was getting pretty close;
the question that I asked him
    I should not have, I suppose

'cause I asked why the digging
    was straight East from our house
when the drainfield was up North;
    it upset my tired spouse.

He said to mind my business,
    it was right there on the map
and I thought I'd better let it be
    so I let it go at that.

Next day he filled the tractor up
    then began to dig again,
he dug the hole out wider;
    not a sign of tank within.

The front lawn was now history,
    with a crater in its place
big enough to hold the house
    and there was not a trace

of drain pipe or a septic tank,
    the third day he gave up
and said to call the plumber back
    and have him try his luck.

The plumber soon arrived;
    in a flash, or even less,
the location of the septic tank
    was where you might have guessed.

It was North toward the drainfield
and it seems my trusty spouse
had used the map that showed the tank
at his dear old mama's house.

Another tank of fuel was used
to fill the crater in
and I still am planting grass seed
where a nice lawn once had been,

but we both learned one good lesson
'sides where the septic tank is at;
"be sure that when you start to dig
you're not using mama's map!"

This is how we went to school when I was little. My older sister, Clara, drove the horse (Prince); my sister, Mamie, rode beside her, and I rode on the bottom right behind Prince's tail. We went to Wortman School about two miles from our farm. (In Tripp County, South Dakota). Old Prince would really take us home! I suppose he knew he would get some feed when he got there. Clara had trouble holding him back sometimes. One time, he started out and Mamie wasn't in the buggy yet. Some of the bigger boys that rode horseback rode hard and got us stopped. Clara got Prince turned around and went back and got Mamie.

—Gen (Storms) Fast
Clearfield, South Dakota

Some Things Never Change

She saw him one day at the sale barn café
    and they say it was love from the start;
she thought he looked good in his black Stetson hat,
    and his wink stole the young maidens heart.
It sure wasn't long until wedding bells rang,
    she was sure that her life would be great;
but she got upset on their way to the ranch
    when he stopped to let her get the gate.

The poor gal was sure that the cowboy'n life
    was the kind that she'd seen on TV;
a big, fancy house with a cook and a maid,
    but she soon learned it wasn't to be.
The house was a shack with an outhouse out back
    and the water was hauled in a pail;
but we are aware that true love can endure
    and it seems she adjusted quite well.

She learned to raise gardens, to cook and to can,
    and would help her dear cowboy outdoors
with fencing or feeding or putting up hay,
    and was willing to help him do chores.
It wasn't the life that she once dreamed about,
    but she loved her dear home on the range;
and when she thought back to the day that they wed,
    there is only one thing she would change.

She still loves that cowboy as she did back then
    and she still likes him in his black hat;
he takes her out dancin' and still winks at her,
    and the sight of him sure takes her back
to the night they were wed.....such sweet memories,
    there is only one thing that she hates:
when they go somewhere and come back to the ranch,
    he still stops to let her get the gates!

Commercial Truckers Can't Be Beat

When your husband is a rancher
    and makes a living off the land;
you try to make your dollars stretch
    and save 'em where you can;

And there's one expense my husband
    thought that surely could be cut:
the cost of hauling cattle,
    he'd just buy a good used truck.

The dealer saw us coming;
    he had just what we needed,
it was a good used cattle truck
    "and at a bargain" he conceded.

It took some time to get it home
    (hubby had to find the gears);
but thought of all the dough we'll save
    in just a few short years!

We parked it 'till we needed it,
    and before you know, 'twas spring;
time to haul the pairs out West
    but we couldn't start the blasted thing!

It only needed batteries
    (they don't give those things away).
We finally got it started,
    and bed the trailer down with hay.

He slowly backed that great big truck
    towards the loading chute;
it took more than a dozen trys
    ...to direct him was no use.

He finally got 'er all lined up,
    we run some cattle up the chute,
then loaded the first compartment
    when some floorboards busted loose.

It took some time to patch that up,
    he was getting somewhat sore;
the salesman failed to tell him
    that the trailer needed a new floor.

He finally got her headed out;
    and oh my, he was proud;
then halfway down our driveway
    that semi got real loud!

Have you ever heard a Detroit Motor
    when the muffler's fallen off?
The blue smoke was a bellering
    when the motor began to cough.

I could go on about that truck,
    and about its great demise;
but to give you all the details
    perhaps would not be wise.

That semi is not history,
    along with all the bills
that it cost when we once owned it;
    a great big box would fill.

We're still a-strugglin' on the ranch,
    to try to make ends meet;
but we learned one real good lesson:
    "Commercial Truckers can't be beat!"

My parents, Gladys and Vern Denny, lived on a farm near Ainsworth, Nebraska, during the Depression. They had a little girl, Dorla, and a baby, Terry. Terry had been very sick and as a consequence, my mother had not left the place for some three months. That was not all of her troubles, however, as it was apparent that the bank was going to foreclose on them and they were in the process of planning an auction sale to pay off what they could. In lieu of the inevitable, they butchered a hog and a beef so they would hopefully have enough to eat for awhile. Mother undertook the monumental task of canning all of the meat. The day the last canner full was shut off, Dad asked Mother to go with him into town. Because Terry was finally able to travel and it had been so long since she had been to town, she set the canner aside to cool and accompanied Dad. When they returned home, Mother asked Dad to take the cooled jars of meat from the canner to the cellar and put it next to all the rest. Dad quickly returned with the horrible news that there was nothing left in the cellar. While they were in town, someone had stole the entire contents. All they had out of the hog and beef was the canner full that was left in the house while they were in town.

—Mary Mulligan
Wood Lake, Nebraska

In the summer of 2000, we had 8 cow/calf pairs stolen from a pasture. The next summer, we had 16 calves stolen off the cows in the same pasture. Although we were upset, we felt our troubles were small compared to two of our neighbors who also had cattle stolen from neighboring pastures that same summer of 2001. One fellow was laid up with a broken leg, and one was away taking cancer treatments. The following poem was written with reference to this.

The Cattle Thief

I'm writing this poem for a stranger
    I sure hope it's for no one I know;
and I pray that in time you're forgiven
    for you sure have been stooping quite low.

Did the cattle you stole from our pasture
    help you in paying your bills?
Or did you just take 'em for something to do
    or perhaps for the sake of a thrill.

Are you planning to have a good Christmas?
    There is plenty of reason you should
for them cattle you stole probably brought quite a lot
    as the market is up pretty good.

You certainly had no expenses
    like the rest of the cattlemen have
and you never lost sleep when a norther came in
    and the heifers had started to calve.

And the one guy you stole cattle from
    must have seemed like an easy prey;
of course, his cancer had come back again
    and he had to go away

takin' treatments, and them other guys
    were probably nowhere about;
but then you surely knew about that
    I'm sure you had checked it all out.

I know that those fellows did nothing to you
    so it couldn't have been for revenge;
to think that there's people as low as you are
    makes most of us worry and cringe.

I really feel sorry for those you stole from,
    but I feel so much worse for one other;
the person who's heart would break if she knew;
    .....I really feel bad for your mother.

There is a poem by Scott Redington entitled "Reflection On Riches" that I have heard performed by Wyoming Poet, Echo Roy, in which there is a line referring to how the poor folks are doing. That line was in my thoughts one day when I was trying to come up with a poem for my annual Christmas letter. I had been sick for several days; the news that day was that the hog market was the lowest it had been since the Great Depression; and several of our friends and neighbors had been forced to sell out because of the economy. I was in a dismal mood and was looking out of my living room window when the following poem came to me.

How the Poor Folks are Doing

As I was writing my Christmas letter,
   I tried gathering up my thoughts,
I thought of all my blessings
   and folks, I counted a lot..

But as I sifted through my memories
   trying to write some Christmas Cheer;
I just stopped writing and wondered
   how the poor folks are doing this year.

I always write about the grandkids;
   we think they're pretty sweet;
they like our country way of life....
   .....to them it's quite a treat

to come here and help with the cooking,
   and to go with the men feeding hay;
they just love it outside, and I wonder:
   how are the poor folks doing today.

They're a-livin' in some crowded city
   in a high-tech style of life;
a-workin' a job that they hate every day,
   and drowning their sorrows at night.

Of course, they make real good money,
    and out here we barely get by;
but we're rich if we count all the good things
    in our old fashioned style of life.

We all know that the cattle market
    has hit an all-time low;
and expenses have hit an all-time high
    as the politicians blow

'bout how good they've made the economy
    ....don't look too good out here;
but from here I stop and I wonder
    how are the poor folks doing this year.

A cold front came in yesterday
    and we got some snow last night;
those trees on the lane look so pretty
    all covered with frost, sparkling white.

There's a hawk circling over the meadow
    as the cattle graze quietly by;
a soft breeze is turning the windmill
    against a cold morning's gray prairie sky;

I feel "rich" as I gaze from my window
    and thank God for the good life out here.
From my home in Dakota I wonder:
    how are the poor folks doing this year.

Here to Help us Out

Old McDonald had a farm
  in which he had much pride.
He worked real hard from sun to sun,
  his family by his side.

He raised good crops and livestock
  and planted groves of trees;
had milk cows, hogs and chickens;
  sold cream and eggs and cheese.

Then here came Uncle Sam who said
  he'd planted too much grain,
and taxed him for his income;
  he did not dare complain.

(We all have heard the speeches
  from folks in politics,
how they only want to "help us out";
  we all know it's a trick.)

They taxed his land and livestock,
  his tractors and his truck;
taxed him for the things he bought;
  his protests brought no luck.

Now Old McDonald's left the farm
  he took a job in town.
His buildings sit decaying;
  the barn is falling down.

His neighbors, too, have left their farms
  and sold to wealthy men
who use them for a place to hunt;
  as we question: "Will it end?"

One wonders as we drive along
a lonely country lane:
Is family farming gone for good;
will it return again?

One thing that we can count on
that'll never change, no doubt;
when Uncle Sam comes visiting
he's just here to "Help us out!"

*Someone had to help us out, according to Frances Creech of Octavia, Nebraska.
This was in the gumbo in the Missouri Valley near Yankton, South Dakota
(on the Nebraska side) on August 16, 1923.*

That Little Shed Out Back

One thing I remember well
   about my childhood days;
were trips to my dear grandma's
   where we would go and stay.

She had no running water;
   she had no R. E. A.
She had an old pump organ
   and my, she sure could play.

Her house was lit with kerosene;
   she cooked on an old range;
but of all the old appliances
   there's just one thing I would change.

The one thing really needed
   that my Grandma never had,
the one thing I missed most of all,
   'specially when the weather's bad.

You see, she had an outhouse
   and it was way out back;
we held as long as possible
   before heading to that shack.

In winter it was miserable
   to climb upon the seat;
we'd brush the frost or snow off
   'cause the roof, it always leaked.

In summer there were wasps and flies,
   and of course, that awful odor;
one could always find a catalog,
   but it wasn't there for orders.

It is fun to be nostalgic
   and wish that we could be
way back in time when we were young
   and repeat those times, you see.

But one thing I will never miss
   as I am thinking back;
is the times I had to make a trip
   to that little shed out back!

Photo taken of South Dakota Homesteads in 1908. Each homesteader received a quarter section of land. They had to establish residence on that quarter (called proving up). This is where four different homesteaders set their shacks in an area where four quarters joined in the center. Often they did this and shared a well in the center. This one appears to have a communal outhouse in the center!

I know, most of you called it "the chamber (pot)" but at our house we called it "Charlie!!" When I went to high school in Gretna, Nebraska, and met friends who were used to electricity and bathrooms that flushed and all that. It was a real treat to stay overnight at their house, so I invited Marie Mangold to come and stay a weekend at my house. When it came time to go to bed, Dad sorta quietly said to me: "Charlie's in the closet." Now that meant to me that Charlie was not still on the porch and needed to be taken upstairs on the way to bed. Unfortunately, that is not what it meant to Marie! (Remember - she had a bathroom at her home) She thought "Charlie" was the hired man or something!

Some time later, she told me that she had not slept a wink for fear that Charlie might come out of the closet!

—Lois (Ruff) Gottsch
Elkhorn, Nebraska

Mortgage One Good Wife

When the banker pays a visit
   to check your inventory
the way he values assets, folks
   is quite a different story

than the values placed upon them
   by the one who sells insurance;
and if them two would switch their jobs
   it would really make a difference.

The first thing that the banker does
   is try to claim your land;
he says it's really not worth much
   but on the other hand

he needs it for security.....
.....with the cattle market down;
but he can't loan you cash on it
   'cause it is only ground.

The value of your cattle
   is the price the packer pays;
your machinery....it's not worth a dime
   it's seen its better days.

You can't borrow on a good old horse,
   you can't borrow on your wife;
your house ain't worth a tinker's damn
   and neither is your life.

BUT HERE COMES YOUR INSURANCE MAN!
   He sings a different song;
and says that horse is worth a lot!
   You knew that all along.

He says you need a policy
   just in case it meets its fate;
and you'd better have a BIG one
   on your kind and loving mate.

He says she's worth a million
    if you figured up the cost
of hiring folks to do her work;
    why, she'd really be a loss!

And what about those buildings
    that the banker said was junk;
if disaster took just one of them
    you really would be sunk!

And if lightning hit some cattle,
    the loss would be immense;
you have got a hundred thousand
    in just windmills, tanks and fence.

When that agent finished tallying
    it looked like we were wealthy;
the way he figured assets
    made our finances quite healthy.

So I hope you get my point
    in them two switchin' jobs, you see,
'cause if bankers sold insurance
    not very much you'd need.

And if Insurance Agents
    made the agriculture loans,
we'd all be driving brand new cars
    and living in new homes.

We'd be looking pretty prosperous,
    and live a "rich man's life";
instead of buying life insurance,
    you'd just mortgage One Good Wife!

Women who lived in sod houses often said that the only color or item of decoration in those drab homes was their red geraniums. I was thinking of that when I wrote the following poem:

The Little Red Geranium

The church that day was crowded,
    it was filled clear to the brim;
the organist was playing
    her favorite old hymns.

I thought how folks would miss her.
    For the most of ninety years
she'd been doin' things for others,
    and the thought brought me to tears.

Pretty flowers lined the altar,
    but among the large bouquets
sat a little red geranium
    and it looked so out of place.

I wondered how it got there
    but I didn't wonder long
for the service was beginning;
    first a prayer, and then a song.

Then the pastor started talking
    and he left the Speaker's Stand;
he picked that scraggly plant up
    and held it in his hand.

He said he went to see her
    just before she passed away,
and she gave that plant to him
    with instructions for this day.

She first told him a story
    that he'd tell to us today,
'cause she asked him if he'd share it
    just before she passed away:

Her folks came West to homestead
    when she was just a girl,
And her mama got so lonely
    in this strange and foreign world.

But one day a kindly neighbor
    brought a red geranium.
She gave it to her mama
    ....and that was to begin

a long and lasting friendship;
    then every year towards fall
her ma would take starts from it
    and she would share them all

with others that were lonely,
    or sick, or needed care;
she would take a red geranium
    and leave it with them there.

She said her mama told her
    it reminded her of God,
how He made us in His image
    from a little clump of sod.

And with a little kindness
    and a little bit of care,
plants, like His love, could multiply
    and grow for us to share.

She said when she was living
    in a soddy in the hills,
she always had geraniums
    blooming on the big wide sills.

Red was the only color
    in her drab and dingy home
reminding her that God was there
    and she was not alone.

Then came those awful thirties
    when the hills were parched and brown;
those pretty red geraniums
    were the only things around

that seemed to keep on growing,
    and how she loved them so;
and kept right on a-givin' them
    to visitors when they'd go.

Then wartime came and took
    her only son, so brave;
it was a red geranium
    that she planted at his grave.

Now her life on earth is over,
    but before she went away,
she started many little plants
    to give to you today.

Just little red geraniums
    descended from her mother's;
through years it's been her joy
    to share with many others.

She hopes you all will take one
    and you'll have it in your home;
then when you're feeling lonely
    you will know you're not alone,

'cause flowers fade and wither;
    seasons come and seasons end,
but your plant will live and grow
    if you share it with a friend.

We all were taught a lesson
    at the funeral that day:
the greatest love we can receive
    is the love we give away!

L to R: Gladys, Clarice & Eleanore Klein; their Grandmother, Flora Hobson; and their mother, Coral Hobson Klein, in front of their Sod House door.

This poem was written on March 27, 1935, by my Grandmother, Blanche Hanson, who lived on a farm North of Glenham, South Dakota. About the poem, she wrote: "I wrote this poem during one of our worst dirt storms when visibility was nill. It was an unbelievably dark dust storm, exactly like a snow blizzard, only just dirt."

Saga of the Dust

The dust storm is raging, it roars o're the Plain,
oh, give us an old fashioned blizzard again!
These twisted up thistles that with the dust blow,
oh, give us a blizzard of old fashioned snow.

How black the horizon and dreary the view,
I wish it would snow, that I wish it would do.
The dust is so thick on the benches and sill,
we eat it and drink it, we sure get our fill.

Our bushel allotment we've eaten and more,
oh, I wish it would rain...I wish it would pour.
We know it's the year Nineteen thirty and five,
but we soon will forget it if buried alive.

The dust and the gravel sails over my head,
it spreads a drab coverlet over my bed.
Cheer up! It may rain so we nearly will drown
and send the grass shooting to hold the dust down.

If we just grin and bear it and put on a smile,
the corner may turn, it may rain after while.
The sky is all dark and the sun sheds no glow,
oh, please come again, you blizzard of snow!

A dust storm rolling up near Gregory, South Dakota - 1934

We had a bad year in 1934. Our mother died on April 17, and Mary (now Mrs. Martin Jorgensen) was only five years old, so I stayed home to help Dad with the younger kids. One day my brother Leo was in the field with a disc and four horses and one of those black blizzards came up and he couldn't see a thing. There was no way to tell where he was or where he was going, but the horses took him home.

—Gen Fast
Clearfield, SD

My friend, Harley Furrey, gave me the idea for this poem. This happens every year in every neighborhood.

Mother's Day Branding
(the male version)

Oh blessed is the lady who invented Mother's Day,
    a time to show our gratitude in kind and thoughtful ways.
But why does it have to be that same Sunday every May?
'Cause that's the day our neighbor has his annual branding day.

Of course one has to help, that's what all good neighbors do;
    but it upsets the little wife and puts her in a stew.
Each year I hear the same thing how I shouldn't go at all
    but this neighbor always helps with our roundup in the fall.

I try to make excuses but that seems to make things worse;
    I invited her to go along, but it only made her curse
when I told her that's a way she could spend the day with me,
    and she could help his wife out with so many men to feed!

I've told her that I care for her much more than any other,
    but she shouldn't get upset 'cause she is not my mother.
I sensed a little anger when she shook her fist at me,
    and told me I'd be sorry for my insensitivity

'cause next month on Fathers Day she told me she'd be gone
    and she hoped that I'd feel awful when I spent the day alone.
I let her think she won the war, but just 'tween you and me
    I heard about this roping and that's where I'll probably be!

I'd better smooth things over, guess I'll take her out to dine;
    there's a salebarn bar-b-que tomorrow noon at Valentine.
I'll tell her that she's still my gal and that should pave the way
    'till next year when the neighbor has his branding Mother's Day!

Mother's Day Branding
(the female version)

Oh blessed is the lady who invented Mother's Day,
   a time to show our gratitude in kind and thoughtful ways.
But why does it have to be the same Sunday every May?
'Cause that's the day our neighbor has his annual branding day.

Of course, one has to help, that's what all good neighbors do,
   but it upsets this little wife and puts me in a stew.
Each year I try to tell Pa how he shouldn't go at all
   but this neighbor always helps us with our roundup in the fall.

Pa tries to make excuses, but that seems to make things worse.
   He invited me to go along, but it made me want to curse
when he told me that's a way he could spend the day with me,
   and I could help the wife out with those men she has to feed!

He told me that he cares for me more than any other
   but I should not get upset 'cause I am not his mother.
I got a little angry when I really shouldn't be,
   and I told him he would pay for his insensitivity,

'cause next month when it's Fathers Day I said that I'd be gone
   and I hoped that he'd feel awful when he spent the day alone.
But when I thought I'd won the war, he winked and grinned at me
   and said that there's a roping and that's where he probably be.

He said he'd smooth things over and he'd take me out to dine
   at a salebarn bar-b-que tomorrow noon at Valentine!
He tells me that I'm still his gal and that should pave the way
   'till next year when the neighbor has his branding Mother's Day!

The "Soddy" in the 40's. This was the home of Coral Hobson Klein.

Coral Hobson married George Klein in 1918 and began their married life together on a ranch North of Valentine. One spring a severe wet snow collapsed the roof of the cow barn killing most of their cattle. Coral's domestic chores were considerable. Corn cobs or cow chips were collected and wood chopped and carried into the house to fuel the cook stove, and in winter, the heating stove too. Water was pumped by hand or a windmill and was also carried into the house and the "slop" pails were carried out. Once I complained about the never ending winds and Coral told me: "When one is raised to depend on the wind to provide water for yourself or your cattle, you learn to be happy the wind is blowing!" In addition to caring for a growing family, and the never ending domestic chores, Coral raised a large garden; canned and stored the harvest to feed her family as well as hired help; raised chickens to eat and for eggs; milked cows and with the help of the children, hand turned the separator. Some of the cream was churned into butter for their own use. The skimmed milk was carried out to the hogs, and cream, eggs and chickens were taken into town and sold. For most of the farm and ranch women this income was used for groceries, clothing and household supplies.

—Jo Ann K. Klein
Hidden Timber, South Dakota

The Vocation

Many, many years ago
our neighbors had a boy;
he was the only child they had
so of course, their pride and joy.

They spent much time a-pondering
what their fine young lad would be;
they knew he'd turn out special
and had big plans for him, you see.

They knew he was too honest
to be a lawyer or politician;
perhaps he'd be a surgeon
or a high-paid obstetrician.

They thought he had real talent
so they hoped he'd play pro-ball;
he could probably work most any sport
'cause to them he had it all.

He would never be a banker
'cause he had too much ambition;
he might end up in Nashville
for he was a good musician.

Now, they are really nice folks
but they have the darndest luck;
their little guy is now grown up
and he's out there driving truck!

But folks, it sure could be much worse
than what a trucker's job would be;
he could have hit rock bottom
and have a job with the D.O.T.

Do you suppose these two are headed for the polls?

My grandmother, Etta Goodin, was born in Wichita, Kansas, in 1871. The family moved to Nebraska, and she worked at Ft. Niobrara for the General Miles family, where she met William Johnson, who was an aide for General Miles. They were married in Valentine in 1893. She was an army wife for five years. One baby died and is buried in Arlington Nat'l Cemetery. After his discharge, they returned to Cherry County where they ranched South of Valentine. They lost three children within six months time, the oldest only nine. When women were finally allowed to vote, Will didn't approve. After he left to vote, Etta hitched up her horse and buggy, gathered all the women in the neighborhood, and they went to vote. Some were reluctant, but Etta convinced them of their rights. Needless to say, the men were surprised.

—Ruthie Johnson Harms
Valentine, Nebraska

The Calving Book
(also known as "The Big Oh-No!")

There are sins in this old world of ours
    that would make the devil curse;
each time you think you've heard it all
    well, here comes something worse.

There is one thing that a rancher's wife
    must never, never do;
it's the absolute worst thing of all;
    it could be the ruin of you.

I must admit I've come real close
    to crossing that fine line,
but it happened one Spring day last year
    to a real good friend of mine.

You could hear her husband holler
    from a couple miles away;
and when I heard just what she'd done
    all I could do was pray

that somehow she'd find forgiveness,
    for that poor old gal had took
a dirty shirt and washed it.....
    and it contained his *calving book*!

The Heinous Husband Award

There's a quite prestigious contest,
    and you're about to hear
how awards are made at Christmas,
    with one winner every year.

They list all women's Christmas gifts,
    then all the gifts are scored;
the giver with the most points wins
    "The Heinous Husband Award!"

In this National sponsored contest,
    there is a real good chance
that the winner of each fine award
    makes his living on a ranch.

Of all the fine submissions,
    a committee picks just two;
from the two they tap a winner
    and here's examples of a few:

There's Jack and Dee, the newlyweds,
    their first Christmas together.
they lived in North Dakota,
    where folks get some awful weather.

Jack was the top vote getter
    back in nineteen-ninety-two;
it seems he bought his lovely bride
    four-buckle overshoes.

Vernelle got post hole diggers
    from old Ervy, whom she loves;
in her stocking Christmas morning
    was some elk-hide fencin' gloves.

An automated vaccine gun
    was presented to Doreen;
her hubby won in ninety-three
    they thought that gift quite mean.

In ninety-four, Link won that year;
    his gift cost quite a lot;
and when poor Debbie opened it,
    folks say she looked quite shocked!

She had pointed to her silverware
  and said that's what she needed.
He misconstrued her gentle hint
  .....on that he soon conceded!

The gift was well-intended;
  but, oh my, she was torqued,
when Christmas morn, the gift she got
  was a new four-tined pitchfork!

Last year my husband won it.
  they say he topped the lot;
he sure blew a lot of money
  'cause a Bobcat's what I got.

My friend had got a new blue fox,
  I thought I'd like one too;
he explained: "Fox don't make loaders,
  but the Bobcat folks sure do!"

So, I got this fine contraption,
  (what I wanted was a coat)
and 'cause that Bobcat was all mine
  ......I had to sign the note!

Last year my stepson won it.
  I'll tell you folks, it's sad,
'cause he looks just like his mother
  but he acts just like his dad.

See, his wife had often told him
  not to littler 'round his chair;
she found it Christmas morning
  .....a new trash can sitting there.

It had a bow taped on it
  with a note inside that read
that he was gonna get her more
  but got a new remote instead!

So, if you get a gift sometime
  that's not to be adored;
you might submit the giver for
  the "Heinous Husband Award!"

Blanche & Engval Hanson, 1925, after working outside all day.
In the background is a work & saddle horse, Skeeter.
To the right, and almost out of sight is their sod house,
and peeking from behind Engval is his young son, Harry (my father).

Diary Entry dated Wednesday, May 30, 1934:

Decoration Day. Dry with hot winds. Pa fixed the calf pasture fence and turned the five calves in there. There are some Russian thistles there for them to eat, the only green thing visible. I patched all day. It seems the more I patch the more I find to patch. The men went down in a draw to plant potatoes. I will go to town tomorrow. I have to limit the two weeks grocery list to two dollars.

—Blanche Hanson (1892-1973)

Windmill on the Prairie

If I could paint a picture of the finest place on earth,
it would never be of buildings, pay no matter what they're worth.
There'd be no canvas covered with a village, neat and quaint;
a windmill on the prairie is what I'd choose to paint.

Now, you may think it silly that anyone could see
beauty in a windmill, but they mean a lot to me.
Like a lighthouse to a sailor, they're a symbol of the West
of life that's free and easy and a lifestyle that's the best.

To me there's nothing better than to be out there with God;
smelling clover-scented grasses or fresh raindrops on the sod.
To hear the rustling of the trees, the lowing of the herds;
and watch a hawk a-circling low, then chased away by birds.

A friend to man and beast alike, they never cease to work,
bringing forth the fresh cold water from far beneath the earth.
When evening shadows lengthen, like a tower in the night,
a windmill on the prairie is such a wondrous sight.

You can have the Eiffel Tower or the Vatican in Rome;
sky scrapers in the cities, or the fanciest of homes.
The simple, upright beauty that will put them all to test
is a windmill on the prairie when the sun sets in the West.

This poem was written by my grandmother, Blanche (Arnold) Hanson. She grew up and lived her entire life on the South Dakota prairie. She wrote a lot of poetry about her life and about South Dakota.

To a Wild Rose

Oh, I'd rather have a Wild Rose
grown by ever loving hands,
than all the fragrant beauty
of strange and foreign lands.
You'll see a lot of beauty
wherever you may roam;
but none compares with a Wild Rose
for a Wild Rose means home.

This is a poem by my great-grandfather Ben Arnold (1844-1922), and is a favorite of mine. Anyone who lives on the prairie loves the song of the Meadowlark as much as the beauty of the prairie flowers.

The Meadowlark

After the winter so drear and long,
The first to cheer us with his song;
From early morn 'till nearly dark
Is our own Dakota Meadowlark!
I always love to hear him sing
I watch and listen every spring;
And when I see him in field or park
I say: "God bless you little lark!"

About the Author

Yvonne Hollenbeck's poetry is an expression of the way of life as a cattleman's wife on the South Dakota prairie. The material for her poetry is often found through everyday experiences, together with a reflection on the life of pioneer women.

Yvonne and her husband Glen own and operate a cattle and quarter horse ranch, in South Central South Dakota, which was founded many years ago by Glen's granddad, Earl Hollenbeck. As she reflects on her life, she is ever mindful of the hard work and dedication of the pioneer women in her family who did without so that her life might be better. She is the first generation in either her or her husband's family to live an entire lifetime with running water, indoor plumbing, and electricity.

Hollenbeck has been a featured poet at many of the Cowboy Poetry Gatherings in the Western United States and Canada including the National Cowboy Poetry Gathering at Elko, Nevada. She is also recognized as a popular entertainer for civic functions.

In addition to her writing, Yvonne is involved in music, quilting, and community activities. Author of two books and tapes of cowboy poetry, Yvonne Hollenbeck considers poetry her favorite hobby, second only to her grandchildren.